To/

Les

with thanks for all

the good times

TEXTUAL NARRATIVES AND A NEW METAPHYSICS

Drawing extensively upon recent developments in post-phenomenological philosophy, especially 'the textual turn' exemplified by Paul Ricoeur, Jacques Derrida and Maurice Merleau-Ponty, this book explores the role that textual narratives have in the possibility of reasonably affirming the intelligibility of the world. Shorthouse reveals how textual narratives can play a primary role in affirming rational meaning in a continuing hermeneutical process.

Offering a radical new approach to metaphysics, Shorthouse demonstrates that rational meaning is ontologically grounded in terms of a transcendental viewpoint or perspective. It is this grounding which transcends the language and the self in a hermeneutical movement towards the affirmation of rational meaning. Revealing that the critical characteristic of reading a narrative is rhythm, Shorthouse explains how each narrative has a rhythmic structure, or prose rhythm, in relation to its semantic and figurative characteristics, activity and mood. Two key questions are explored: what kind of rational unity may be affirmed which does not close or suspend reflection? and what kind of linguistic mediation may generate an extralinguistic, or transcendental element in establishing an ontological grounding for this affirmation? The response to both these questions is presented in terms of textual sonority, where Shorthouse draws upon, and develops, Maurice Merleau-Ponty's notion of sonorous being.

ASHGATE NEW CRITICAL THINKING IN PHILOSOPHY

The *Ashgate New Critical Thinking in Philosophy* series aims to bring high quality research monograph publishing back into focus for authors, the international library market, and student, academic and research readers. Headed by an international editorial advisory board of acclaimed scholars from across the philosophical spectrum, this new monograph series presents cutting-edge research from established as well as exciting new authors in the field; spans the breadth of philosophy and related disciplinary and interdisciplinary perspectives; and takes contemporary philosophical research into new directions and debate.

Textual Narratives and a New Metaphysics

RAYMOND T. SHORTHOUSE

Ashgate

Aldershot • Burlington USA • Singapore • Sydney

Published by
Ashgate Publishing Limited
Gower House
Croft Road
Aldershot
Hants GU11 3HR
England

Ashgate Publishing Company
131 Main Street
Burlington, VT 05401–5600 USA

Ashgate website: http://www.ashgate.com

British Library Cataloguing-in-Publication Data
Shorthouse, Raymond T.
  Textual narratives and a new metaphysics. – (Ashgate new
  critical thinking in philosophy)
  1. Storytelling 2. Literature – History and criticism
  I. title
  809

Library of Congress Cataloging-in-Publication Data
Shorthouse, Raymond T.
  Textual narratives and a new metaphysics / Raymond T. Shorthouse
      p. cm. – (Ashgate new critical thinking in philosophy)
  Includes bibliographical references.
  ISBN 0-7546-1610-X
    1. Metaphysics. 2. Narrative (Rhetoric) 3. Rhetoric – Philosophy.
    I. title. II. Series.

BD111.S53 2001
110–dc21

                                                              2001041270

ISBN 0 7546 1610 X

Typeset by PCS Mapping & DTP, Newcastle upon Tyne.
Printed in Great Britain by Antony Rowe Ltd, Chippenham, Wiltshire

Contents

Preface

This book has its origin in my childhood, when my father awakened a love of poetry and literature within me. Many years later, as a parish priest in the Church of England, I learned to appreciate the rhythms of language in the Anglican liturgy, and consequently to be interested in their significance in particular modes of language. I am grateful for the privilege of conducting services of worship in many parishes over a period of thirty years, and the opportunities I was given to pursue my interest during my time as Director of Christian Studies in the Diocese of Derby.

The study is based upon my PhD thesis at Warwick University, and among those who have helped me in my studies, I wish to thank, in particular, my supervisor, Martin Warner, for his support, patience and critical attention. I also wish to thank my examiners, Peter Poellner and Richard Kearney, for their encouraging comments and suggestions. Also, I wish to thank my wife, Sylvia, for her patient, constant support in all my ministry and studies.

Raymond T. Shorthouse

Introduction

The more self-forgetful the listener is, the more deeply is what he listens to impressed upon his memory. When the rhythm of a work has seized him, he listens to the tales in such a way that the gift of retelling them comes to him all by itself. (Walter Benjamin, 'The Storyteller' in *Illuminations*, p. 91)

In his essay, 'The Storyteller', Walter Benjamin recalls that 'the art of story telling is the art of exchanging *experiences*'. It is, according to Benjamin, the decline of this art, which he laments, that is manifested in the earliest symptom of the rise of the novel at the beginning of modern times. In contrasting these two art forms, he identifies a significant difference in a confrontation of novel and story in the slogans 'meaning of life' and 'moral of the story'. Drawing upon the work of Georg Lukács, he claims that the quest of the novelist is to grasp the temporal unity, or 'meaning of life'.

The decline of storytelling coincides with the breakdown and fragmentation of temporal unity and 'meaning of life' of the grand narratives which set the scene for the storyteller until the beginning of modern times in the seventeenth and eighteenth centuries. The art of exchanging experiences in the craft of writing then becomes informed by the quest for the 'meaning of life' around which the narrative moves. In relation to this quest, my aim is to focus upon what may be discerned as a common element in the oral tradition of storytelling and textual narratives. The above quotation relates the significance, according to Benjamin, of 'the rhythm of a work' in relation to memory and the retelling of stories. It is in the ability to listen to the story in terms of self-forgetfulness and being seized by a deep rhythm that the storyteller is able to memorize and consequently develop the art of exchanging experiences. This is the rhythm of the listener's state of being as she actively responds to the story in an imaginative grasp in a moment of self-forgetfulness. There is a profound rhythmic resonance whereby the listener's memory is imprinted with the experience of the story. In this sense, the textual narrative is analogous to the memory of the storyteller. That is, the ontological rhythm is mediated by the rhythmic structure and patterns of the text.

This rhythmic structure, or *prose rhythm*, is the mediation of an ontological foundation of *Sonorous Being* by which there may be an affirmation of temporal unity and 'meaning of life' in relation to unconstrained questioning and provisional explanations – an affirmation of meaning founded upon an affirmation of the reader's self-identity within a process of what Paul Ricoeur calls, a 'hermeneutics of suspicion'. Textual narratives play a significant role in the affirmation of self-identity in the continuing process of interpreting and sharing experiences in the contemporary world of fragmentation and

1

dissemination; a world in which grand narratives are being discarded, and all metaphysical notions rejected.

My main concern is to present a new metaphysics radically different from all traditional attempts in Western philosophy to satisfy the human desire for absolute knowledge of the Other – a metaphysics which provides a grounding for rational thought in a hermeneutical process open to a horizon of rational probability. In contrast to the traditional perspective of epistemological acquisition, this is a metaphysical grounding for an appropriation of the Other's viewpoint, an appropriation whereby there may be an affirmation of self-identity with respect to the rational meaning of that perspective. In terms of textual narratives, it is the reader's imaginative grasp of the 'implied' author's viewpoint grounded in her rhythmic condition of being mediated by the prose rhythm of the narrative. This rhythmic condition of being, or Sonorous Being, is the transcendental, metaphysical source of affirmation.

In the first three chapters, I address the key question of *presence* in Continental philosophy. My examination of the notion of 'presence' in the phenomenological and ontological philosophies of Husserl and Heidegger, with particular reference to the contrasting critical perspectives of Derrida and Ricoeur, aims to show that, in this context, the problem of 'presence' is not fundamentally concerned with a question of conceptual unity with respect to the meaning of particular words, but with the relationship between the figurative characteristics of metaphor and narrative, and the semantic structures of sentence and discourse. That is, it is the reader's imaginative grasp of the figuration of the text in relation to reflection upon the narrative which must be examined in addressing the question of presence. This grasp, it will be shown, is the mediation of a grounding of the relationship in a rhythmic, sonorous condition of being. It is a relationship which Ricoeur terms a *primordial dialectic*, first used in his theory of metaphor, and developed in his theory of narrative between the world of the narrative in terms of its textual configuration and the self-identity of the reader in terms of rational description and explanation. It is an attempt to show that the question of presence is not fundamentally a question of conceptual unity but the unity of the world which the reader imaginatively appropriates and inhabits, and that sonority and rhythm play a key role in this notion of unity.

To this end, my analysis in these initial chapters draws particularly upon Ricoeur's theories of metaphor and narrative in identifying, firstly, the significance of sound in relation to image and subsequently developed as prose rhythm as the key characteristic of the objective nature of the text in terms of the intrinsic structural stress patterns, and not simply the rhythms of intonation and emphasis of individual readers. I will show how metaphor and narrative may be analysed in terms of the objective textual mediatory characteristics of a figurative and semantic dialectic; the figurative being grounded in symbolic structures which mediate activity in terms of its ontological roots, sonority and rhythm being essential features of this activity.

Analogous to participating in liturgical activity with symbols playing an ontological mediatory role, the reader imaginatively participates in the active world of the text by means of the symbolic rhythmic structures of metaphor and narrative. Unity, or presence, is achieved in the rhythmic drive to inhabit the world of the text. But the movement is dialectically related to a continuing process of interpretation with respect to reflection upon the semantic structures of the text, which is a 'hermeneutics of suspicion'. Therefore, the question of the possibility of affirmation through the mediation of sound and rhythm takes account of 'suspicion' which cannot be suspended.

But what is the nature of this rhythm with regard to the relationship between 'affirmation' and 'suspicion' ? Chapters 4, 5 and 6 are devoted to the development of the notion of prose rhythm by identifying and addressing four ontological issues. The first issue is concerned with the way the reader appropriates the viewpoint, or perspective, of the world of the narrative. How does the reader imaginatively become immersed in the narrative to participate in that world? How does she grasp the unity of that world in terms of its temporality and identity? These questions are focused, in addressing the first issue, upon the relationship between ontological unity and sound. In relation to the former, my analysis draws upon Ricoeur's notion of narrative identity, and with respect to the latter I introduce the notion of prose rhythm, and give literary examples to illustrate the role of rhythm in poetry and narrative, based on a development of Maurice Merleau-Ponty's notion of *phonetic gesture* as an important feature of the 'lived' body. My aim is show the way in which the reader's grasp of the narrative identity is rooted in an ontological sonority which is mediated through the 'lived' body. The body must be understood phenomenologically in the way it is consciously mediated at different levels, and objectively in terms of its physical materiality. In other words, ontological sonority as the fundamental characteristic of the reader's grasp of ontological unity in terms of narrative identity is mediated in the rhythmic resonance of the physical body, and phenomenologically mediated in rhythmic sound patterns.

The issue of ontological unity and narrative identity is pursued in terms of the second with respect to Merleau-Ponty's notion of *corporeal intentionality*. My concern is to relate the work of Ricoeur in *Time and Narrative*, in which he analyses the process of grasping the world of the narrative in terms of *mimetic configuration*, with a corporeal understanding of intentionality; furthermore, to show that this intentionality involves a dialectic between what Merleau-Ponty calls *particular* and *operative* intentionalities. That is, with respect to reading, the attention is focused upon particular parts of the text in the process of grasping the meaning, the unity of the narrative. But this particular attention is made possible by the background of the unfolding world which the reader imaginatively inhabits but of which he is not directly conscious. These are two levels of dialectically related intentionalities. In relation to the mediatory textual characteristics of rhythm, prose rhythm is shown to be the mediation of operative intentionality with the rhythmic characteristic of the iconic focus of metaphor being the mediation of particular intentionality. The significance of the latter is the concrete nature of metaphor and, according to Ricoeur's interactive theory, its power of redescription in terms of new meaning that captures the reader's attention. Again literary examples are given to illustrate the dynamic process of corporeal intentionality.

The grasping of the narrative by the reader is a dialectical process between the reader and the world of the narrative; between self-reflection and the temporal perspective of the narrative. In becoming immersed in the story, the reader's self-identity is disturbed in an imaginative appropriation of the narrative identity. It is a process of habitation which disturbs the reader's state of being. Analogous to Benjamin's claim that listening to a story is being seized by the rhythm of the story, this disturbance of the reader's state of being is rhythmic in a profoundly ontological sense, and is the grounding of the primordial dialectic in Sonorous Being. For this reason, the mediation of this rhythmic sonority in the textual characteristics of the narrative is evident in the structural rhythmic texture of the poetic/narrative mode. Chapter 5 is devoted to providing this evidence in addressing the third ontological issue, which is the relationship of Sonorous Being to the primordial dialectic.

In an analysis of poetry in terms of the variety of rhythmical beat my aim is to show that, for the most part, although prose rhythm is essentially based upon stress patterns, there is not a dichotomy between these two forms. That is, they are part of a rhythmic spectrum which may be discerned in prose narratives, particularly in the relationship between metaphor as the textual focus of attention and the discursive, descriptive passages which, to a great extent, form the background in the reader's grasp of the narrative. In this sense, poetic rhythm relates to the metaphorical iconic focus, and prose rhythm to the background of the imaginative world of the text. The latter may resonate beyond the reader's conscious attention in his physical body and state of being. The rhythmic beat of the former is the dynamic of the reader's grasp of the iconic focus of unity, the grasp of the metaphor's concrete image, which vehemently generates a new meaning to provoke the reader's self-reflection. Textual rhythm is examined in a number of examples to show that the rhythmic structure of the text may be seen to mediate the ontological grounding of the primordial dialectic in the relationship between the metaphorical rhythmic beat and the stress patterns of prose rhythm. As part of this examination, I also show that textual rhythm mediates emotional states, activity and – significantly with respect to rhythmic anticipation - the mediation of temporality.

The issue of presence forms part of my analysis of the third ontological issue in relation to appearance. The question is, how does the rhythmic texture mediate the primordial dialectic of sonorous being? How does sonorous being appear? My aim is to develop the work of Heidegger and Ricoeur with regard to the ontological notion of within-time-ness, with some acknowledgement of Heidegger's later seminal notion of the 'rift' as the appearance of the figure. The key question is, how does Being appear without being grounded in an unquestioned transcendental subjectivity? Or rather, how can Being appear if its unity, its meaning, is not open to an horizon of continuing interpretation? Does not transcendental subjectivity inhibit such a hermeneutical process by being fundamentally unquestioned? It is my contention that Ricoeur and Heidegger have not gone far enough in addressing this key question, and that the rhythmic structure of the text in particular provides the way of doing this. It is because prose rhythm resonates at the 'edge' and beyond consciousness that it evades the criticism that it is tied to transcendental subjectivity. The appearance of Sonorous Being in terms of its primordial dialectic therefore is mediated in the textual rhythmic structure.

Chapter 6 is a further development of the primordial dialectic with respect to the fourth ontological issue, which is the understanding of this dialectic in terms of Self and Other. Here the philosophical notion of 'Other' is used to refer to narrative identity, and particularly to what Ricoeur calls the 'who' of the narrative. My aim is to analyse the relationship of the reader to the viewpoint or temporal perspective of the narrative in terms of a dialectical relationship between the reader's Self, and the Other-than-Self of the narrative; that is, the reader's imaginative grasp and habitation of the Other's viewpoint, of a different and new meaning which may be affirmed and yet never be free from questioning. In other words, the dialectic between Self and Other in the process of habitation is a dialectic of affirmation and suspicion. To this end, my analysis draws upon the work of Ricoeur, particularly in *Oneself as Another*, and Emmanuel Levinas. With respect to the latter's rejection of any possibility of comprehending the Other, I take a radically different approach in showing that the fundamental metaphysical issue is not to affirm an understanding of the Other but to appropriate the perspective of the Other. The reader appropriates the viewpoint of the Other, the 'who' of the narrative, and does not attempt to face the Other in an act of comprehension. It is not a question of a metaphysical foundation for epistemological acquisition of the absolute, but a metaphysical grounding for inhabiting the rational viewpoint of the Other.

In my analysis of the dialectic between Self and Other, I investigate the way in which the rhythmic structures of a text may mediate the ontological sonority of the reader's grasp and habitation of Another perspective which is seemingly incomprehensible and therefore beyond the reach of any act of affirmation. This particularly refers to tragedy and the apparently absurd perspectives which seem to defy any attempt at understanding the singularity of a particular viewpoint. An example of the latter which has occupied, among others, the thoughts of Kierkegaard and Derrida, is the Biblical narrative of Abraham's sacrifice of his son Isaac. In a detailed analysis of the text, I attempt to demonstrate how the rhythmic structures of the 'Authorized

Version' of the Bible may be seen to mediate a dialectic of Self and Other in terms of affirmation and suspicion. That is, the text may be shown to mediate a sonorous resonance in the act of reading whereby the reader is driven to affirm a provisional meaning which possesses a teleological dynamic, giving the reader a conviction of reasonable hope to persist in a continuing process of interpretation.

Chapters 7 and 8 focus upon two principal features of my analysis. More than anything else, the reader's grasp of the narrative and habitation of its world is a work of the imagination. It is the creative imagination which generates a hermeneutical process in which the reader is responsive to a horizon of meaning provoking self reflection and a redescription of self-identity. Chapter 7 is devoted to an analysis of the creative imagination by first looking at Ricoeur's reinterpretation of Kant's notion of the *productive* imagination in his *Critique of Judgment*; and to develop this notion to show that its dynamic is grounded in the 'lived' body and Sonorous Being.

The theme of Chapter 8 is the second principal feature of the analysis. This relates to the issue of relationship between fantasy and reality. With respect to the role of the creative imagination, is there a way of affirming the meaning of the narrative in terms of reasonably opening the reader to new perspectives of understanding the world and himself? Is there a way of reasonably validating such meaning in contrast to the imaginative flights of fantasy? If written narratives may indeed play a key role in the quest for meaning in a world of fragmentation and dissemination, is it possible that there may be *reasonable hope* that such meaning may be affirmed in the historical context of unconstrained questioning and provisional explanations? Or is it inevitable that, in this sense, reasonable hope must be abandoned in favour of pragmatic conventionality? In this chapter, I analyse validation as the basis of reasonable hope in terms of Ricoeur's notion of attestation as the basis of a conviction of probability. That is, attestation analogous to juridical witness and testimony, and evaluated by practical wisdom as specified through the Aristotelian notion of *phronêsis*. It is my aim to show that attestation and reasonable hope are fundamentally the work of the creative imagination grounded in the rhythm of hope of Sonorous Being and mediated in the dialectic between affirmation and suspicion.

Sonorous Being is a metaphor for the metaphysical source of affirmation in the reader's grasp and inhabitation of the world of the narrative. In the final chapter, I present a profile of this new metaphysics, based upon my analysis in the preceding chapters, to show that this is a transcendental grounding, mediated through the rhythmic structures of textual narratives, which generates an impulse of rational probability in relation to an horizon of unconstrained questioning.

Chapter 1

The Question of Presence

The Vulgar Notion of Presence

The ordinary, or vulgar notion of presence is the understanding that individual and corporate entities may be affirmed as being at hand on the basis of sensible, empirical evidence. An object, for example, a table, to be accepted as being present must be subject to sensate experience of sight and touch. Complex objects, such as a computer, may require a more critical demonstrative process but fundamentally the basis of any attempt to affirm that the object is present is sensible evidence. Even when the part played by language in rational descriptions of simple or complex demonstration of presence is recognized, the vulgar notion still retains the view that empirical experiences lies at the foundation. That is, it is the linguistic capacity of words and sentences in terms of any statement or description to provide ostensible reference as indications and expressions of empirical experience; it is the semantic characteristic of language to refer beyond language to entities and situations in the world that provides the medium for giving expression to presence.

Although this vulgar notion of presence does not go unquestioned in ordinary discourse, for example in the recognition that sense experience is susceptible to distortion and misinterpretation, it is, nevertheless, to all intents and purposes for everyday life, accepted as a sound basis for human perception and knowledge. Any discernable error of judgment regarding the presence of an object will be subjected to a disciplined rational analysis based upon sensible experience. The juridical system, for example, places circumstantial evidence under suspicion of judgment in contrast to clearly demonstrated eye-witness reports. And yet, philosophical debate has always raised radical epistemological questions about these matters. How is it possible to know what it is that sense experience is derived from? Can sense experience alone be the foundation for an epistemological judgment with reference to an object? Is the question of presence fundamentally an epistemological issue? What is the basis, if any, for affirming that something is present? If affirmation is not possible, does this mean that there is no way of knowing what if anything is present at hand? Or does it mean that there will always be an element of suspicion about the objects of thought and language? Is it only if there is a source of affirmation beyond sensible experience and the process of rational thought, a source beyond language, that the presence of things may be known? That is, is it only if there is a metaphysical foundation for knowledge of the objective world that presence may be affirmed? However, in the debates of modern Western philosophy, since the major work of Kant's *Critique of Pure Reason* in which he exposes the fundamental problem of the empiricist's epistemological view of sensible experience, and attempts to demonstrate the foundation of transcendental idealism in the *a priori* categories of rational thought, there has been a development in the radical questioning of any metaphysical trace.

The Problem of Presence – Three Perspectives

In attempting to address this critical issue of presence, three possible approaches present a choice of perspective for analysis. Firstly, there is the cognitive process of rational thought. Does the key to the question of affirming presence, as Kant proposes, lie with the structuring and capacity of the rational mind? Or, secondly, should the critical perspective be focused primarily on the question concerning the possibility of direct or immediate access to the objective world in terms of sensible experience, intuition or some ontological condition which may be analysed and defined? Thirdly, there is the linguistic medium which may be understood to relate the first to the second. Is the critical clue to the question of affirmation to be found in the nature of language which may reveal either endemic suspicion, or the possibility of a hermeneutical movement towards affirmation of presence? The three perspectives cannot, of course, be separated, and each will involve an acknowledgement and account of significant issues relating to the other two. Therefore, in taking a linguistic perspective for this study it will be necessary to give careful consideration to the critical questions raised by processes of rational thought and its relationship with the world. Obviously, the latter immediately provokes the question, what is meant by 'the world', but this will be taken up in due course.

Metaphysical Assumptions

The fundamental problem of presence is the seeming impossibility of rationally affirming the absolute unchanging unity of particular entities on the basis of the ceaseless flux of temporal experience. To make the statement, 'There is the table', is acceptable in terms of the vulgar notion of things, but if the word 'table' in this sentence is an ostensible reference for the presence of the object, how is it possible for the word to affirm that presence if it is subject to a changing play of sensate experience in relation to positionality and temporal flux? If it is claimed that empirical experience cannot be the foundation of the word, or concept, but takes its capacity to affirm presence from the *a priori* structures of the rational mind – that the mind, as it were, is metaphysically constructed – this not only raises fundamental questions about the notion of presence, if, as according to Kant, there is no possibility of the rational mind deriving the source of its ability to conceptualize from empirical experience, but also provokes radical questions about the seemingly unquestioned metaphysical assumptions with respect to the *a priori* categories of rationality.

Language and Phenomenology

My approach to language in this study is in terms of a phenomenological analysis, and not grammatical structures. That is, it is the relationship of language to the way the conscious mind perceives objects as phenomena, how they appear in consciousness. The significance of this will be made clear in due course. What is important is that empirical experience is taken up into a givenness whereby a critical analysis may begin the process of questioning. This does not mean that consciousness, or some level of consciousness to be determined, may provide a kind of ultimate foundation in the manner of the Cartesian *cogito ergo sum*,[1] but it is the conscious mind which questions that is the location of givenness.[2] Empirical experience with respect to rational thought is mediated through the phenomenological structuring of the conscious mind. The sensate experience of an object, such as a table, in terms of sight which will include colour, size, shape, etc., may only be the object of rational thought through the mediation of appearance in consciousness: this is a table; the table is square and has four legs; it is a dining table. It is the appearance as the mediation of empirical experience of the object which is the givenness where the questioning must begin. To this end, the nature and structure of this appearance provokes the initial stage of the analysis.

Husserlian Phenomenology

In the context of the development of phenomenology, it is the appeal of Edmund Hussel 'to the things in themselves' which has provoked the debate, particularly with respect to Martin Heidegger's ontology, around the issue of presence. Presence for Husserl – or rather the essence of pure being, or the thing-itself, 'the judged state of affairs [*Urteilsverheit*] (the affair-complex [*Sachverhalt*]) 'itself'[3] – raises the question of what genuine grounding, what evidence can be taken for knowing that it is there. It is a question of uncovering what Husserl calls the final sense of science. As already noted, the task is to begin with the given, not with the Cartesian rational subject. The given, according to Husserl, is consciousness in which the objective world appears, and is the grounding of the *cogito*. What the given reveals is the problematic of knowing the thing-itself. If it is the grounding of the *cogito* in contrast, for example, to the transcendental Cartesian or Kantian subjects,[4] then what is it that ensures a continuing affirmation of the presence of the thing-itself in consciousness?

Husserl is at pains to demonstrate that sense experience cannot provide genuine evidence for knowing the object itself. For example, consciousness is always subject to the modalities of being in the world. There are the spatial modalities whereby an object is experienced from particular positional perspectives. For example, a house cannot be viewed from all sides at once. Furthermore, the position determines the appearance of the building. Also, as Husserl writes,

> (For example: the 'modalities of being', like certainly being, possibly or presumably being, etc.; or the 'subjective' – temporal modes, being present, past and future.) This line of description is called *noematic*. Its counterpart is *noetic* description, which concerns the modes of the *cogito/* itself, the modes of consciousness (for example: perception, recollection, retention), with the modal differences inherent in them (for example: differences in clarity and distinction). (*Cartesian Meditations*, p. 36)

Thus, there is no such thing as pure consciousness in relation to ordinary experience. In other words, the naïve or natural attitude, which implicitly tends to disregard the critical part played by spatial and temporal modalities of perception, takes empirical experience of tables, chairs, doors, and all entities in the world at hand as genuine evidence of the things-themselves, and consequently may be subject to sensible illusion. For example, a person walks into a room and sees an object for the first time and is uncertain what it is, and therefore moves to different positions concluding that it is indeed a table. There is of course some awareness of the influence of positionality, or perspective, but the dominant concern, for the most part, is to gain sufficient empirical evidence to make the judgment that the object is a table. But, according to Husserl, such judgments cannot be grounded in sense experience since the intentional, constituting nature of consciousness plays a significant and determinate role in the judgment.

Husserl: Expression and Indication

What, therefore, is the ground of consciousness? This is a question that for Husserl arises from his fundamental concern with the ground of science. That is, on what foundation is the logic of science grounded? To this end, in pursuing his phenomenological analysis, he defines consciousness as structured by phenomenal images in terms of Expression (*Ausdruck*), and Indication (*Anzeichen*);[5] that is, images as signs both expressing meaning and indicating certain objects or states of affairs. In his analysis of these meaningful signs, Husserl is concerned to make clear that both expression and indication are related to motivation and intentionality of the thinking subject. For example, in *Logical Investigations*, Volume 1, he writes

> A thing is only properly an indication if and where it in fact serves to indicate something to a thinking being.
> (*Logical Investigations*, Vol. 1, p. 270)

For this reason, it is the 'thinking being' that takes priority, and is essentially disclosed in the meaningful expressive nature of consciousness. In other words, consciousness is meaningful expression in terms of the synthetic activity of intuition and intentionality. Furthermore, meaning is expressed even when there is no object present, and, therefore, in this sense, no indication. There are, Husserl claims, two expressive acts which he calls *meaning conferring* and *meaning fulfilling*. He writes,

> But if the object is not intuitively before one, and so not before one as a named object, mere meaning is all there is to it. If the originally empty meaning-intention is now fulfilled, the relation to an object is realized, the naming becomes actual, conscious relation between the name and the object at hand.
> (*Ibid.*, pp. 280–81)

Again, priority is given to expression, to meaningful intentionality of the conscious subject in the living present. Indication is integrally related to expression but separate with regard to its primordial grounding in the voice of the speaking subject.

In effect, and in the course of his analysis, Husserl separates Expression and Indication, and, with respect to the former, privileges intentionality and intuition. Consequently, in Husserl's phenomenological analysis, the question is prompted, is not the presence of the thing-itself made dependent upon a metaphysical presupposition?[6] In his attempt to seek a foundation for the logic of science in an access to the presence of the thing-itself through the givenness of the appearance of meaningful signs, does he not go beyond the given? This is a fundamental criticism of Jacques Derrida in *Speech and Phenomena*,

> We have thus a prescription for the most general form of our question: do not the phenomenological necessity, the rigor and subtlety of Husserl's analysis, the exigencies to which it responds and which we must recognize, nonetheless, conceal a metaphysical presupposition? Do they not harbor a dogmatic or speculative commitment which, to be sure, would keep the phenomenological critique from being realized, would not be a residue of unperceived naïveté, but would constitute phenomenology from within, in its project of criticism and in the instinctive value of its own premises? This would be done precisely in what soon comes to be recognized as the source and guarantee of all value, the 'principle of all principles': i.e., the original self-giving evidence, the *present* or *presence* of value to a full and primordial intuition.
> (*Speech and Phenomena*, p. 5)

Derrida criticizes Husserl's endeavour to separate expression from indication. That is, the meaningful sign system in terms of language, which for Husserl is grounded upon the living presence of the speaking subject.[7] This is why the voice is so important for Husserl. In his commitment to his central aim to disclose the grounding of the presence of pure being, his analysis reveals the fundamental problem of affirming presence in relation to the sign system in terms of indication. For example, there is the problem, as referred to above, of the modes of being in relation to objects and states of affairs. Any description of an object or state of affairs is subject to the particular mode of being, and therefore these descriptions are constantly subject to the possibility of multiple modalities, and, consequently, may be explicitly or implicitly polysemic. Also, there is the problem of temporality which will be considered below. Therefore, indication as the basis of rational statement and description cannot be the indication of the presence of pure being. A *meaning fulfilled*, according to Husserl, cannot be grounded in the word or description, but in the *meaning fulfilled intention* of the speaking subject. The essence of consciousness is Intentionality in terms of the synthetic activity of primordial intuition.[8] It is this grounding that Derrida claims reveals a metaphysical presupposition in Husserl's commitment to the transcendental ego.

Husserl: Presence and Time

A particular and crucial focus of Derrida's criticism is set out in *Speech and Phenomena* in relation to Husserl's *Phenomenology of the Consciousness of Internal Time*.[9] A key issue which Husserl identified is, how is it possible to affirm the unity of the thing-itself, the unity of pure being, on the basis of its givenness in the phenomenological structuring of consciousness when this givenness is endlessly subject to the changeableness of experience; a changeableness not only of spatial positionality but temporality? Consciousness is always consciousness in time; the living present is always in relation to the past and the future. The present continually moves from a past which was the present to a future which will be present. How then is the object presented, or rather re-presented in the mediation of the linguistic sign system? The answer to this question requires a careful study of the concepts of *vorstellung* in the work of Husserl and Derrida.[10] Husserl's fundamental attempt to resolve the problem of temporality with respect to intentionality is by means of the concepts of *retention* and *protention*.[11] Derrida is critical of these concepts and claims that this attempt at reaching the purity of the present by compounding the past and the future with the present in effect contaminates that purity and reveals that presence is linguistically derived from nonpresence. He writes,

> One sees quickly that the presence of the perceived present can appear as such only inasmuch as it is *continuously compounded* with a nonpresence and nonperception,

with primary memory and expectation (retention and protention). These nonperceptions are neither added to, nor do they *occasionally* accompany, the actually perceived now; they are essentially and indispensibly involved in its possibility.

As soon as we admit this continuity of the now and the not-now, perception and nonperception, in the zone of primordiality common to primordial impression and primordial retention, we admit the other into the self-identity of the *Augenblick*; nonpresence and nonevidence are admitted into the *blink of the instant*.
(*Speech and Phenomena*, pp. 64–5)

In his hermeneutical philosophy, Paul Ricoeur takes a more sympathetic view of Husserl's attempt to take account of temporality with the concepts of retention and protention, which relates to his own work on symbols that prepare the way for his theory of metaphor. It is his work on symbols that is profoundly influential in his analysis of the *iconic moment* of metaphor[12] which is of central importance with respect to the immediate and presence; in particular, it is Ricoeur's analysis of the *productive* imagination, drawing upon Kant's *Critique of Judgment*[13] in relation to the iconic moment of metaphor that calls for critical examination, especially from a Derridean perspective.

What is important for Ricoeur is Husserl's seemingly radical step in understanding the nature of unity in his quest to resolve the aporias of temporality. In chapter 2 of *Time and Narrative*, Volume 3 – 'Intuitive Time or Invisible Time? Husserl Confronts Kant' – Ricoeur develops his thought in relation to this radical step and narrated time. What is significant for Ricoeur is Husserl's attempt to define the appearance of time in consciousness, or *time-consciousness*. With respect to temporality, it is the difference between lived time, intuitive time or *internal time-consciousness*,[14] and objective time, clock time or the series of *temporal nows*, and the relation between these two. Ricoeur commends Husserl's radical discovery regarding lived time. Taking Husserl's example of sound to describe a unity of duration, and not the unity of the object, he writes,

Husserl's discovery here is that the 'now' is not contracted into a point-like instant but includes a traverse or longitudinal intentionality (in order to contrast it with the transcendent intentionality that, in perception, places the accent of unity of the object), by reason of which it is at once itself and the retention of the tonal phase that has 'just' (*soeben*) passed, as well as the protention of the imminent phase.
(*Time and Narrative*, Vol. 3, p. 26)

Ricoeur acknowledges that the 'one after the other' is formulated by Kant[15] as necessary for the appearing of temporal-objects, Husserl's zeitobjekt.[16] Nevertheless, he is concerned to make clear the difference of continuance that he understands in Husserl's analogous description of sound:

By continuance, however, we are to understand the unity of duration (*Daurerinheit*) of the sound ... 'It begins and stops, and the whole unity of its duration

(*Dauereinheit*) of the sound … it begins and ends, 'proceeds' to the end in the ever more distant past'. There can be no doubt – the problem is that of duration as such. And retention, merely mentioned here, is the name of the solution that is sought (*Ibid.*, pp.26–7)

According to Ricoeur, this continuance is the effect of retention, or primary remembrance that makes possible the perception of the 'one after the other', the series of now-points; a unity of duration whereby the present and the recent past mutually belong to each other as an enlarged present.

> The present is called a source-point (*Quellpunkt*) precisely because what runs off from it 'still' belongs to it. Beginning is beginning to continue. The present itself is thus 'a continuity, and one constantly expanding, a continuity of pasts'. Each point of duration is the source-point of a continuity of modes of running-off and the accumulation of all these enduring points forms the continuity of the whole process. (*Ibid.*, p. 30)

But what is the ground of this source-point? Even though Husserl takes the unity of the process in terms of duration as the primary effect of intentionality, or rather splits intentionality between its entwined primary and secondary modes,[17] it is, nevertheless, the intentionality of the transcendental subject, the *a priori* subject, which may in this ultimate sense be compared with the Cartesian and Kantian subjects. It is still, therefore, the Husserlian transcendental ego which grounds this understanding of presence. And so, Derrida's and Ricoeur's criticism of this unquestioned subject remains. Both are concerned with taking the givenness of linguistically structured temporal consciousness, and resist any attempt to posit a constituting metaphysical subject as the grounding of presence. Such *a priori* grounding must inevitably constitute a 'closure'[18] whereby presence understood as pure being is negated. What then for Ricoeur is the ground of this unity of the process of duration? Does he attempt to define a ground? If not, how is this unity possible? Must not any attempt include an extralinguistic reference, and consequently transgress the given of linguistically structured consciousness?

But Derrida's insistence upon the givenness of the phenomenological structuring of the sign system whereby presence is endlessly deferred challenges Ricoeur's attempt to incorporate an extra-linguistic dimension to this givenness. For Derrida, the production of meaning is intra- linguistic in the sense of the Saussurean notion of *difference*, but since there is no transcendent grounding for meaning it is always deferred beyond the phenomenological horizon[19] of meaning. According to Derrida, the two processes are one in what he terms *Différance*. The notion of *Différance*, however, is indefinable and far more complex than this semantic understanding.[20] Does not Derrida's disciplined commitment to the givenness of the linguistic sign system, particularly in its written mode, remain faithful to a refusal to collude with a metaphysics of closure, and consequently reveal a fundamental failure of Ricoeur's project in embracing an extralinguistic transcendent dimension? To put it another way, does not Ricoeur seem to endeavour to have it both ways? That is, does he not attempt to remain within the linguistic medium and yet define a linguistic process in the Husserlian notion of unity of duration by means of a dynamic that is clearly extralinguistic? What kind of linguistic process is this? What kind of unity is achieved? What kind of extralinguistic dimension is it that does not transgress the givenness of linguistically structured historical consciousness?

Ricoeur and Derrida: A Different Perspective on Language

In attempting to address these questions, it is important to understand that the critical departure from Husserl, by Ricoeur and Derrida, is a departure from his perspective on language. For example, Husserl's concern with the sentence, 'The table is there', is with the conceptual unity of the table in terms of grounding its presence in the transcendental consciousness of the voice that speaks the sentence. In other words, for Husserl this is consciousness that is not essentially linguistically mediated. For Ricoeur and Derrida, the concern is with the language sign system of which the sentence is a part. Meaning is produced within the dynamics of the system. Therefore, presence, in this sense of the possibility of univocity, for Ricoeur, and absence, in terms of the illusions of univocity, for Derrida, is mediated through this sign system. That is, the possibility of linguistically, and therefore consciously, affirming the presence of the table, the thing-itself, or the impossibility of linguistically affirming the presence of the table, is revealed in the written text, the *trace*, of the linguistic sign system as the necessary mediation of historical consciousness. For Ricoeur and Derrida, metaphor is a key characteristic of this sign system, which for Ricoeur transcends the system in the creative power of the imagination, but for Derrida reveals, through deconstruction, the fundamental disseminating process of the system and a semantic *retrait*.[21] Their critical departure from Husserl involves a radical break with the primary conceptual view of traditional Western philosophy. But for Ricoeur, this is the way to affirm conceptual unity, or at least in a teleological sense of a movement from suspicion to affirmation,[22] within a hermeneutical spiral, a continuing interpretative process of understanding (*Verstehen*[23]) and explanation in which metaphor plays a fundamental role. Whereas, within Derrida's perspective, conceptual language calls for endless deconstruction, or rather it is subject to deconstruction through its metaphoric *trace*.[24]

My aim in taking a critique of Husserl from Ricoeurean and Derridean perspectives has been to identify the given as the site of the analysis of the problem, and to discard any assumptions or prejudgments, especially unquestioned metaphysical ones. My intention is to demonstrate that the affirmation of presence does involve a metaphysical dimension made accessible within the site of the given and not the other way around. To this end, drawing upon the work of Ricoeur and Derrida, the question of presence must include a critique of the fundamental role played by consciousness in constituting the presence of the thing-itself. Therefore the central concept of intentionality understood as the meaning conferring characteristic of consciousness is taken up in my critique of Ricoeur and Derrida, taking account of their critical departure from Husserl's development of his theory of meaning with respect to language in terms of expression and indication. For both of them, the site of the given is consciousness linguistically structured through and through. Although Husserl attempts to affirm presence in the unity achieved through expression of the 'now', it is the intentional, synthetic unity of the transcendental ego that is the grounding of this unity for Husserl. In this sense, language is not basic to the question of presence, whereas for Ricoeur and Derrida it is primarily the mediation of the linguistic sign system that determines the question of presence. It is in their diverging response to this question that a critical focus for defining the essential nature of the problem of presence is provided. Ricoeur's attempt to show how the affirmation of presence may be achieved in a hermeneutical movement from suspicion to affirmation in which univocity of rational explanation and description is based upon the metaphoric/narrative mode of language provokes the radical question from a Derridean perspective, what kind of univocity or unity is this?

Heideggerian Ontology and Presence

This question takes the analysis and the investigation of the problem of presence to an ontological level in Ricoeur's endeavour to show how metaphor functions in the linguistic mediation of the ontological grounding of rational discourse. What is at stake is an understanding of the unity of being as that unity which makes possible a hermeneutical movement from suspicion to affirmation of presence. According to Ricoeur, metaphor is central to this movement. Ricoeur and Derrida begin with a valued recognition of Husserl's appreciation of the ontological issues, for example, his critical understanding of the important role played by modes of being in the world, and his attempt to demonstrate a rational affirmation of the object's pure being. But they are also critical of his seeming forgetfulness and hiddenness of the ontological problematic.

Husserl's concern to separate expression from indication as the way to affirm presence grounded upon the expression of the living presence of the voice, on the one hand, is an endeavour to acknowledge the ontological significance of the subject made known in the voice, but, on the other hand, is a failure to question the subject with respect to its ontological grounding.

Upon what foundation does the subject, the transcendental ego, affirm the presence of the voice in terms of expression, and consequently the presence of objects?

This is a question of understanding; the 'upon what' is therefore a question of meaning. What is the meaning of being? What is the meaning of the 'is' in the expression, 'The table is there'? More especially, with respect to the being of the subject, it is a question of the meaning of the 'is' in the sentence 'She is'. But is this a complete sentence? If the 'is' is intended as a predicate, the sentence is incomplete. If treated as an equivalent to 'She exists', then the 'is' cannot properly be construed predicatively, as a number of philosophers have pointed out. It is seemingly to treat the copula 'is' as a predicate, which for a number of philosophers, particularly in the Anglo- American empirical tradition, is to move into the sphere of non-philosophy. That is, the copula cannot be a predicate because it does not assert or affirm a quality or attribute of the subject; it is a mere transitive verbal sign of predication. Therefore, there is no logical, rational basis, in terms of the subject–predicate linguistic structure, for the question of the meaning of being. In acknowledging this critical view of philosophical ontology which, as it were, seeks to understand the pre-conceptual grounding of rational discourse, my aim is not to engage with this debate. It is rather to recognize that Ricoeur and Derrida are part of a tradition, profoundly influenced by the ontology of Martin Heidegger, which consequently wrestles with language. In paying tribute to Heidegger's major work, *Being and Time*, particularly the attempt to expose the meaning of Being, freeing it from the hiddenness and forgetfulness of hermeneutical philosophy tied to direct vision, Ricoeur writes,

> Is this to say that the attempt to escape the dilemma of direct intuition or indirect presupposition can only lead to a kind of hermeticism, considered as a form of mystification? This would be to neglect the labor of language that gives *Being and Time* a greatness that no subsequent work will eclipse.
> (*Time and Narrative*, Vol. 3, p. 63)

In other words, in moving the debate, as it were, beyond the Husserlian notion of intuition as the intentional synthetic activity of the transcendental ego, Heidegger takes the analysis into a radically different mode of language. In so doing, he claims that he is resorting to the necessity of explicitly stating the question about the meaning of Being which has been neglected and ignored since the ontological interpretations of Aristotle and Plato. At the beginning of *Being and Time* he writes,

> On the basis of the Greeks' initial contributions towards the Interpretation of Being, a dogma has been developed which not only declares the question of Being to be superfluous, but sanctions its complete neglect. It is said that 'Being' is the most universal and emptiest of concepts. As such it resists every definition. Nor does this most universal and hence indefinable concept require any definition, for

everyone uses it constantly and already understands what he means by it. In this way, that which the ancient philosophers found continually disturbing as something obscure and hidden has taken on a clarity and self-evidence such that if anyone continues to ask about it he is charged with an error of method.
(*Being and Time*, p. 21)

This note of irony runs through the whole work revealing also the dilemma of attempting such a philosophical analysis with the language of Western philosophical debate which must be challenged and reinterpreted. This is important with respect to the Heideggerian influence upon Ricoeur and Derrida in the way the former seeks to respond to this dilemma in his commitment to metaphor and narrative as the linguistic mediation of the ontological grounding of rational discourse, whereas the latter's admiration is tempered by questioning whether Heidegger has indeed escaped from the assumptions of the tradition he presumes fundamentally to challenge.[25]

From a Heideggerian perspective, the site of the given with respect to the question of presence is not to be defined and analysed by a rational subject–predicate mode of definition which, he claims, is totally inappropriate. The question of presence is the question of the meaning of Being, for Being is presence, and this is to be approached by the givenness of the Being that questions. The site of the given is the Being-in-the-world, the Being-there, *Dasein*, the Being that questions the meaning of Being. This approach is an ontological inquiry primarily concerned with Being, in contrast to an ontical inquiry which is concerned with entities and the facts about them.

Temporality: The Horizon of Being-in-the-world

Heidegger's ontological project is taken up by means of an existential analytic inaugurating terminology in his 'labour of language' to express that which escapes the subject–predicate mode of rational explanation and definition. *Dasein* is a thrown project; that is, it is manifested as Being-there in a condition of thrownness. From this existential perspective there is a key issue of authentic Being subject to fallenness in consequence of being thrown into the world. It is this perspective that leads Heidegger to an ontological understanding of temporality which radicalizes the notion of historical time. It is not simply the question of the intentional synthetic activity of historical consciousness in relation to the past, present and future with respect to affirming presence in the unity of an object, but the attempt to express the temporalizing activity as the condition of being-in-the-world. It is not temporality (*zeitlichkeit*) the noun, but 'to temporalize (*zeitigen*)' the verb, which reveals the radical ontological understanding of historical time.

Although *Being and Time* is devoted to the question of the meaning of Being, and is therefore primarily ontological, it employs an existential analytic particularly with respect to the notion of authenticity and the identification of the crucial difference between *existentiell* and *existential*. The former relates to the facticity of the everyday world, and the entities which are, to use Heidegger's terminology, 'present-at-hand', or 'ready-at-hand',[26] the latter has to do with authenticity or existential freedom, and the notion of fallenness as that condition of being-in-the- world which must be overcome in the striving for authenticity towards the manifestation of the presence of pure Being. *Care (Sorge)* is Heidegger's notion expressing the ontological dynamic of Dasein's openness to authenticity. In this openness *Care* temporalizes *Dasein* in its *ekstaces* of being-in-the-world so that 'Temporality is the primordial "outside-of- itself" in and for itself' (*Being and Time*, p. 377). In contrast to Husserl, who takes the present as the primary focus of temporality, Heidegger's notion of Care makes *Dasein* first and foremost open to the future in the ecstasis of *coming-towards*. The future in consequence gives rise to the ecstasis of the past, the *having-been*, but it is the resoluteness of *Dasein* in Care's anticipation of the future that makes the present the place of action. Heidegger writes,

> Only the Present (*Gegenwart*) in the sense of making present, can resoluteness be what it is: namely, letting itself be encountered undisguisedly by that which it seizes upon in taking action.
> (*Ibid.*, p. 374)

Temporality is therefore the articulated unity of its three modes of coming-towards, having-been and making present.

In his concern to express the ultimate condition of existential authenticity in *Dasein's* openness to the future, Heidegger identifies this as being-towards-death. It is *Dasein's* existential freedom to be in the face of ultimate negation that is the mark of its authenticity. It is in the letting be of *Dasein's* openness to its horizon of temporality, especially being-towards-death, that Being is manifested. In *Being and Time*, Heidegger writes of the spatiality of Being as the way of expressing the manifestation of Being in relation to temporality. It is in the opening of Being towards its temporal horizon that space, understood in existential terms, is the site of the manifestation, the appearance of Being. In later writings, after his *kehre*, Heidegger begins to call this understanding of space as the appearance of Being, 'the clearance, or 'rift'.[27] It is the site opened up by truth; the clearing of the concealment of Being; it is the rift opened up by *Dasein's* letting be, in its struggle to win this open region in which its presence appears.

The purpose of this all-too-brief outline of certain aspects of Heidegger's work is simply, at this juncture, to indicate the ontological perspective that influences and shapes the thought of both Ricoeur and Derrida in their response to the problem of presence. In pursuing Ricoeur's work on metaphor and narrative in subsequent chapters it will be necessary to look more closely at Heidegger's ontology in the attempt to analyse critically Ricoeur's achievement taking into account the Derridean viewpoint. However, what can be said with regard to the aim of this chapter in the attempt to define the problem of presence is that this should address Heidegger's understanding of temporality as the horizon of being-in-the-world, and the appearance, or unconcealment of Being in relation to that horizon.

Heidegger, particularly in his later writings, sets out his understanding of the significance of language as the structure of this horizon, or, expressed in a different way, the house of Being. This coincides with Ricoeur's and Derrida's commitment to language as the phenomenological structure of the given. Therefore, it may be seen that Ricoeur's notion of the text, and Derrida's notion of *l'écriture*, or the *trace*, provide the means for analysing the ontological implications of presence with respect to Heidegger's existential analytic of Being and temporality. To this end, in approaching the question of presence in relation to Ricoeur's notion of the text as the structure of the horizon of Being, which will be shown to be hermeneutical in agreement with Heidegger, the first step will be to examine critically his theory of metaphor as the key feature of the text in particular, to look carefully at the way he attempts to show how rational discourse is ontologically grounded in the iconic moment of metaphor whereby presence may be affirmed within a hermeneutical dialectical movement from suspicion to affirmation. I will take account of the problem of presence from a Derridean perspective in which his contrasting deconstructive theory of metaphor leads to the conclusion that meaning is endlessly deferred. That is, *l'écriture*, as the temporal horizon of Being, is subject to never-ending deconstruction.

Notes

1. In relation to phenomenology, a valuable analysis of the Cartesian *cogito* may be found in Merleau-Ponty's *Phenomenology of Perception*, Part III Chapter 1, 'The Cogito'.
2. The notion of 'givenness' draws upon Heidegger's interpretation of the term *es gibt* (there is, it gives; thus, 'the given'). See *Being and Time*, H7, pp. 26–7. See also Derrida's use of this notion, particularly in *Glas*.
3. First Meditation §4 <51>, *Cartesian Meditations*, Edmund Husserl, pp. 10–11.
4. See chapter 7, 'Kant and Husserl', in Ricoeur's *Husserl: An Analysis of His Phenomenology*.
5. See Husserl's analysis of the *Essential Distinctions* of the term 'sign' with respect to 'indication' and 'expression', Chapter 1, 'Investigation I, Expression and Meaning, *Logical Investigations*, Vol. 1.
6. According to Ricoeur, Husserl's phenomenological reduction is based upon a metaphysical decision (see note 5). See also Emmanuel Levinas's criticism of Husserl's failure to clarify the meaning of 'absoluteness' with respect to the assertion of the 'absolute existence of consciousness' in *The Theory of Intuition in Husserl's Phenomenology*, p. 29).
7. Derrida is critical of Husserl and traditional Western philosophy for privileging the voice, *la voix*, the spoken word, *parole*, with respect to its dominance as self-

presence. This 'apparent transcendence' of the voice is directly linked, according to Derrida, with the concept of truth in the history of philosophy. See *Speech and Phenomena*, pp. 74–9.

8. The immediacy of Husserl's understanding of intuition is grounded in the ontological structures of the transcendental ego's historical presence in terms of intentional consciousness. This contrasts with the variants of Aristotle's account in the *Posterior Analytics* in which he claims that intuition is the originative source of Scientific knowledge (Book II, 19, 100b), and Kant's view that although the immediacy of intuition is situated at the level of sensibility, it is grounded in the *a priori* formal structures of the rational mind (*Critique of Pure Reason*, henceforth *CPR*, B73). See Levinas's illuminating study of Husserl's theory of intuition (as above).

9. In chapter 6, 'The Voice that Keeps Silence',in *Speech and Phenomena*, pp. 82–7, Derrida is critical of Husserl's attempt to demonstrate how the voice is the temporal self-presence of absolute subjectivity. See *On the Phenomenology of the Consciousness of Internal Time* (henceforth *PCIT*) §36, p. 79.

10. See, in particular, Derrida's critical commentary on Husserl's use of *Vorstellung* in chapter 4 'Meaning and Representation' (Ibid.). See also, *§19* ('Repetition') in *PCIT*, p47ff.

11. See *§45*, *PCIT*, p. 308ff.

12. The importance of the iconic moment of metaphor in Ricoeur's thought is rooted in his work on symbols. A valuable essay on the development of this work is 'The Symbol Gave Rise to Thought', by David Pellauer in *The Philosophy of Paul Ricoeur*, ed. Lewis Edwin Hahn.

13. For Ricoeur's view, see 'Imagination in Discourse and Action' in *From Text to Action*.

14. See *PCIT*, Appendix III, pp. 109–14.

15. See Kant's *Critique of Pure Reason*, tr. Norman Kemp Smith, pp. 218–33.

16. See *PCIT*, Appendix IV, pp. 113–14.

17. See *§30*, *PCIT*, pp. 64–6.

18. The concept 'closure' in modern philosophy is used in the contemporary debate about the end of metaphysical discourse. For a valuable contribution see *Delimitations: Phenomenology and the End of Metaphysics*, John Sallis. Also Derrida's important essay, 'The Ends of Man' in *Margins of Philosophy*, and Simon Critchley's *The Ethics of Deconstruction*, Chapter 2.

19. The phenomenological horizon is used in the work of Husserl and Heidegger to describe the way perception is rooted in a 'background' experience. Heidegger relates this to the ontological meaning of the disclosure of *Dasein*; that is, the horizon is defined as the ecstatical unity of temporality. See *Being and Time*, 365, p. 416. This concept has become part of hermeneutical philosophy. For example, see H.G. Gadamer's *Truth and Method*, pp. 302–7.

20. See Derrida's essay, 'Differance', in *Margins of Philosophy*.

21. The word *retrait* in French has a variety of meanings, including withdrawal, retirement and retreat, which Derrida draws upon in relation to metonymy with respect to semantic deferral in his theory of metaphor (see 'The Retrait of Metaphor', *Enclitic* 2.2, 1978).

22. Ricoeur's fundamental view of the human condition runs through his work and is the basis of this teleological movement. In his early existential writings (see *Fallible Man)* Ricoeur claims that there is an originating affirmation which allows

a human being to think and act only through the existential negation which he calls perspective, character and vital feeling. This relationship between affirmation and negation, which is later interpreted in terms of the notion of suspicion, then becomes the primordial dialectic of the hermeneutical spiral in which conceptual thought is affirmed.

23. See Ricoeur's essay, 'Explanation and Understanding' in *From Text to Action*.
24. See Derrida's 'White Mythology' in *The Margins of Philosophy*. According to Derrida there is a continuity between concept and metaphor in which the former is a 'dead' mode of the latter whose image has 'worn away'. In a process of deconstruction the metaphor is unveiled revealing its metonymic characteristic of endless semantic deferral.
25. Derrida raises the question about the 'we' in Heidegger's text ('The Ends of Man', *Margins of Philosophy*). Also in *Of Spirit* Derrida considers the implication of *Spirit (Geist)* in Heidegger's writings.
26. *Vorhanden* and *Zuhanden* respectively. See *Being and Time*, pp. 70–74.
27. In *Being and Time*, Heidegger's concern with presence as the appearance of Being is in terms of place as the site of *Dasein's* letting be. In his later writings, following what is known as his turning, or *Kehre* (see the Introduction to *Basic Writings*, ed. David Farrell Krell, pp. 32–5) he explores the notion of presence in terms of art in which the figure is a clearance, a rift in the concealment of Being. See 'The Origin of the Work of Art'.

Chapter 2

Presence and Metaphor

Presence: Two Critical Perspectives

In my attempt to articulate the problem of presence in Chapter 1, I identified two interrelated critical perspectives. On the one hand, the question of presence is concerned with the problem, particularly revealed in Husserlian phenomenology, of affirming the unity of an object. Unless there is some possibility of grasping the essential unity of an object free from ambiguity and contradiction, how is it possible to affirm rationally that the object is indeed present? In linguistic terms, since from a phenomenological viewpoint language is the medium for meaningful expression of such affirmation, on what basis is univocity achieved? In vulgar terms, the statement, 'The table is there' belies this problem of univocity in affirming the presence of the table. This arises, firstly, from the position of the speaker in relation to the object and the variations in perspective, and the temporal condition in which any statement or description is made. Secondly, the problem of the speaker reveals both the important role of the conscious subject in addressing the question of presence, particularly with respect to the ontological condition of being-in-the-world, and the difficulty of showing how this condition may be seen as the foundation of the affirmation of presence; that is, the problem of showing how the presence of the subject may be ontologically affirmed thus providing the foundation for a hermeneutical process in which there may be a movement from suspicion to affirmation of the presence of objects in the world.

The problem of presence is a question of the phenomenological manifestation, in terms of language, of mediation through rational description, interrelated with linguistic expression of being-in-the-world, and the nature of this interrelatedness. Is the relationship, as Husserl would have it, a privileging of expression over indication which, in effect, means founding indication upon expression? But if Husserl's attempt to found indication upon expression fails by assuming an unquestioned metaphysical foundation, going beyond the givenness of linguistically structured consciousness, is it still possible to show how this relationship may be maintained in and through language? In other words, is it possible to show by a phenomenological analysis of language that the presence of objects may be affirmed, or rather interpreted in a movement from suspicion to affirmation, upon the foundation of linguistic expression of the subject's condition of being-in-the-world? Are there two interrelated modes of language: rational and expressive (or, to use

Ricoeur's term, 'poetic') modes which are not separate but mutually influence and effect change in each other whereby presence may be affirmed? The significant difference between Husserl's understanding of indication and expression, and Ricoeur's rational and expressive/poetic modes of discourse is that the latter involve fundamentally an act of the imagination, whereas Husserlian expression is a mental intentional act, fundamentally cognitive. That is, the contrast is between that which is essentially figurative and that which is essentially conceptual.

Expression: Poetic and Rational Discourse

In the development of Ricoeur's hermeneutical project, it is clear from his early writings, for example *The Symbolism of Evil*[1] and *Freud and Philosophy*, that his interest, which he later pursues, in the poetic mode of language arises out of his ontological investigation of linguistic expression of being-in-the-world. Although he approves of Husserl's attempt to resolve the problem of temporality drawing upon the Bergsonian notion of *duration*,[2] he is critically concerned that this does not address Heidegger's question with respect to the meaning of Being. The ontological question arises from a concern with the condition of being-in-the-world, with the experience of active engagement in which the dominant linguistic mode is expression of immediate response with respect to perception, decision and action, which involves an act of the imagination. Whereas Ricoeur maintains 'rational discourse', which was Husserl's main concern, requires a detour via reflection. It is the means of standing back, as it were, to separate and analyse experience. Although this does not exclude intuition and synthesis, and therefore the Husserlian notion of expression, the essential aspect is reflective analysis.

Husserl's understanding of expression (*Ausdruck*) is based upon the intentional mental act whereby unity is achieved in terms of the intuitive, synthetic process of the act. This assumes a transcendental capacity to achieve an expressed unity as the foundation for scientific, rational analysis. In his attempt to show how this achievement may be accomplished by privileging expression over indication, he remains committed to the view that expression is essentially the way, through speech, the voice confers meaning; and that expression is a mental act essentially of the cognitive processes of the rational mind. In contrast to Ricoeur, the Husserlian notion of expression is not a different mode of language. Although, in the sense of privilege, it may be separated from indication, it is integrally part of rational discourse as the means of its foundation and affirmation of conceptual unity.

Poetic Mode: Ontological Expression

The concern with the expressive/poetic mode of language is Ricoeur's response to the Heideggerian challenge to seek a way of addressing the question of the meaning of Being as an attempt to uncover the ontological foundation of rational discourse. In his analytic of *Dasein* in *Being and Time*, Heidegger engages in a fundamental questioning of the metaphysical concepts, which, according to both Ricoeur and Derrida, Husserl assumes as the foundation of the transcendental subject, in a process he calls *Destruktion*, and which Derrida develops in the notion of *Deconstruction*. According to Heidegger, the task is to destroy the traditional metaphysical/ontological concepts of the post-Socratic Greek philosophers, which remain even in Kantian philosophy where the

> basic ontological orientation remains that of the Greeks, in spite of all the distinctions which arise in a new inquiry.
> (*Being and Time*, p. 49)

The method of *Destruktion* in the analysis of *Dasein* is essentially hermeneutical in a process of uncovering, of disclosing, of letting be whereby *Dasein* may be encountered. It is a task of a disclosive understanding of Being, though non-conceptual.[3] However, Ricoeur is concerned to point out that in *Being and Time*

> from a Heideggerian perspective, the only internal critique that can be conceived as an integral part of the enterprise of disclosure is the deconstruction of metaphysics
> (*Hermeneutics and the Human Sciences*, p. 89)

According to Ricoeur, what Heidegger fails to recognize in *Being and Time* is the fundamental part played by language and discourse in the disclosure of Being. Although the question of language is introduced it remains a secondary articulation. Language is derivative of the ontological structures which precede it. Ricoeur quotes from the passage on language and comments as follows,

> 'The fact that language *now* becomes our theme *for the first time*', says Heidegger in paragraph 34, 'will indicate that this phenomenon has its roots in the existential constitution of Dasein's disclosedness' (SZ 160; BT 203); and further on, 'Discourse is the articulation of what understanding is' (SZ 161; BT 203–4); It is therefore necessary to situate discourse in the structures of being, rather than situating the latter in discourse: 'Discourse is the "meaningful" articulation of the understandable structure of being-in-the-world'
> (SZ 161; BT 204).

Ricoeur then observes,

The last remark anticipates the movement of the later philosophy of Heidegger, which will ignore Dasein and begin directly with the manifestative power of language.
(*Ibid.*, p. 58)

Ricoeur's Theory of Metaphor

The purpose of this brief outline of the significant influence of Husserl and Heidegger upon Ricoeur's work is to introduce his theory of metaphor as the way into understanding the hermeneutical movement from suspicion to affirmation in terms of the creative relationship between the rational and poetic modes of discourse. The problem of presence with regard to the two interrelated critical perspectives identified in Chapter 1 is taken up in the development of Ricoeur's theory of metaphor, and subsequently in narrative theory. His aim is not only to respond to the Heideggerian challenge to uncover the ontological foundation of being-in-the-world, but to show how this foundation is dialectically related to rational discourse in a hermeneutical process; that within this process the possibility of rational affirmation is ontologically founded upon the possibility of the affirmation of the unity of self-identity. Throughout his work, Ricoeur is critical of Heidegger for failing to address the issue of return from the disclosure of ontological foundation to the level of rational discourse. For example, in his essay 'The Task of Hermeneutics' he writes,

> With Heidegger's philosophy, we are always engaged in going back to the foundations, but we are left incapable of beginning the movement of return from the fundamental ontology to the properly epistemological question of the status of the human sciences.
> (*From Text to Action*, p. 69)

It is this return which is evident in the Ricoeurean understanding of the function of metaphor. Metaphor is the focus of the poetic mode of language which brings together in a dialectical relationship the ontological and rational levels of discourse. However, it is important to make clear that in defining the two modes of poetic and rational language, this is not a limitation on the wide variety of texts in which there is an interpenetration of these two modes: those which have a dominant rational mode in, for example, scientific texts, and those with the poetic as the dominant mode, for example, poetry and story.[4] Metaphor is ubiquitous in the sense that it functions in every kind of text and is the focus of the creative dialectic between the rational and the ontological in which the latter is the founding of meaning and the affirmation of presence. But the full effect of the function of metaphor may only be critically examined as the focus of narrative embracing the ontological foundation of self-identity which will be the theme of the next chapter.

Ricoeur's theory of metaphor draws upon the long tradition beginning with Aristotle's *Poetics* and *Rhetoric*,[5] but particularly upon the recent semantic work of literary criticism in the interactive theories of metaphor, especially in the studies of I.A. Richards,[6] Max Black[7] and Monroe Beardsley.[8] The significant feature of these theories is the idea of the creation of new meaning, in contrast to the predominant traditional theories of substitution in which metaphor is essentially an ornamental figure of speech effecting an emotional response and surprise.[9] However, it is the philosophical perspective that Ricoeur brings to these theories with respect to what he calls the primordial dialectic[10] that sets the semantic interaction and the consequent creation of new meaning within a hemeneutical movement from suspicion to affirmation of meaning and presence. It is primordial because it is the way rational meaning is grounded in the ontological condition of being-in-the-world; the latter being the source of which he calls *ontological vehemence* which is the dynamic of semantic interaction creating new meaning. The linguistic mediation of this ontological vehemence[11] is the figurative characteristic of the metaphoric process. It is through the mediation of the figure, the image, and, as Ricoeur describes it, the iconic moment[12] of metaphor that language is dynamically related to the immediacy of the living present and the affirmation of rational unity. This primary characteristic of Ricoeur's theory of metaphor, therefore, is the way into a critical examination of what I referred to earlier as the second critical perspective upon the problem of presence.

Iconic Moment: Ricoeur's Work on Symbols

In examining this iconic moment of metaphor, it is important to be critically aware of its background in Ricoeur's early work on symbols, and the prior development of his thought in existential philosophy. From the beginning, he is committed to what may seem, and will be the subject of closer analysis in a later chapter, the paradoxical aim of affirming existential freedom, that is, Heideggerian authenticity, by way of philosophical reflection upon the condition of fallibility which inhibits and potentially negates affirmation. Drawing upon the work of Gabriel Marcel, Ricoeur identifies a crucial effect of fallibility as the spirit of abstraction, or 'the peril of the objectification' of the human being. According to Ricoeur, this in effect and actuality denies human freedom, by failing to take a holistic approach whereby abstraction and objectification may be understood as rooted in the spiritual and cultural activity of the corporate life world of historical human beings. In other words, there is a non-philosophical background to philosophical reflection in the meaningful structures of the spiritual and cultural features of the *Lebenswelt*.[13] Through continuing human historical activity there is a constant shaping and reshaping of these features. Reflection plays a central part in this hermeneutical process but is not originary. He writes,

> Philosophy does not start anything independently: Supported by the non-philosophical, it derives its existence from the substance of what has already been understood prior to reflection. However, if it is not a radical beginning with regard to its sources, it may be with regard to its method.
> (*Fallible Man*, p.4)

It is this commitment to philosophical method that first led him to explore the problem of myth as that which gives rise to meaning as the expression of the 'Pathetique of "Misery"'. That is, it is the language of myth that reveals the human struggle with the condition of fallibility. Myths then become human stories, the history that informs and structures the spiritual and cultural environment of the *Lebenswelt*. The question for Ricoeur is, how is it possible to engage philosophically with *mythos* in a hermeneutical process? What method may be adopted to interpret the sensible, symbolic manifestations of the pervading *mythos* of the spiritual and cultural milieu? Since philosophical reflection is supported and grounded in these manifestations, how is it possible to achieve affirmation if its very ground is flawed by the aporias of endless struggle to overcome human finitude? Ricoeur is acutely aware of this profound problematic in his work, *The Symbolism of Evil*; and yet, in his dedication to 'lucidity, of veracity, of rigor' in 'the passage to reflection', in *Freud and Philosophy* he responds to his own challenging question,

> Is it possible, I asked, to coherently interrelate the interpretation of symbols and philosophic reflection? My only answer to this question was in the form of a contradictory resolve: I vowed, on the one hand, *to listen* to the rich symbols and myths that precede my reflection, instruct and nourish it; and on the other hand to continue, by means of the philosophical exegesis of symbols and myths, the tradition of rationality of philosophy, of our western philosophy. Symbols give rise to thought, I said, using a phrase from Kant's *Critique of Judgment*. Symbols give, they are the the the gift of language; but this gift creates for me the duty to think, to inaugurate philosophic discourse, starting from what is always prior to and the foundation of that discourse. I did not conceal the paradoxical nature of this promise; on the contrary, I accentuated it by affirming first that philosophy does not begin anything, since the fullness of language precedes it, and second that it begins from itself, since it is philosophy which inaugurates the question of meaning and of the foundation of meaning.
> (*Freud and Philosophy*, p. 37–8)

Symbols: Levels of Consciousness

In Ricoeur's approach to symbols, it is also important to appreciate his phenomenological and ontological perspective in which the linguistic sign system is directly related to what are defined as other levels of consciousness, and particularly to an understanding of intentionality and meaning that is not only self-conscious but corporeal and active. To this end, he acknowledges his debt to Maurice Merleau-Ponty. In *Freud and Philosophy* he writes,

The first corollary to the theory of intentionality concerns the phenomenological notion of one's own body, or, in the language of the later writings of Merleau-Ponty, the notion of the flesh. When asked how it is possible for meaning to exist without being conscious, the phenomenologist replies: its mode of being is that of the body, which is neither ego nor thing of the world. The phenomenologist is not saying that the Freudian unconscious is the body; he is simply saying that the mode of being of the body, neither representation in me or thing outside of me, is the ontic model for any conceivable unconscious. This status as model stems not from the vital determination of the body, but from the ambiguity of its mode of being. A meaning that exists is a meaning caught up with a body, a meaningful behaviour. (*Ibid.*, p. 382)

At the level of Freud's notion of the subconscious, Ricoeur's early work is devoted to the analysis of non-rational symbolic activity at this level. He came to Freud via his work on the voluntary and involuntary will in which, as Walter J. Lowe writes in the introduction to *Fallible Man*, the third part of this early work,

...in and through the interpretation of human experience, he has sought to fashion 'a notion of being which is act rather than form, living affirmation, the power of existing and making exist'.
(*Fallible Man*, p. viii)

What he learns from his 'debate' with Freud is the way a phenomenological approach to the subconscious shows that symbols both conceal and reveal the pre-reflective meanings of human activity. Drawing upon, at the same time as being critical of, Freud's topography of the archaeological symbolic structuring of the subconscious, Ricoeur understands the concealment and revelation of this pre-reflective subconscious symbolic structuring as intrinsic to human activity in the struggle for affirmation in the historical human condition. It is this which discloses the need for a dialectic between an archaeological and teleological opposition[14] within a hermeneutical movement. Symbols have opaqueness which has the effect of concealing the hidden ground of reflection. By means, therefore, of hermeneutical suspicion there may be a process of revealing the arche of language and rational thought in a dialectical relationship with an open teleological horizon of affirmation of new meaning.

According to Ricoeur, the iconic moment is the focus of the linguistic mode of symbolic activity and structuring of historical human activity; it has its roots in corporeal and subconscious activity in the struggle for existential freedom. This aspect of Ricoeur's theory of metaphor is crucial in his attempt to show that the expression of being-in-the-world is objectively grounded. In contrast to the dominantly affective characteristic of the traditional substitutional theory of metaphor, his work on symbols, in terms of its corporeality, provides a way of understanding the materiality and therefore objectiveness of metaphoric iconicity. In this respect, his study of religious symbols and the significant difference between sign and sacrament[15] plays an important part in the development of his theory. That is, symbols do not simply *point to* in the manner of the sign, they are the objective material presence of what they make known. In this sense, the symbol is the concrete moment of the living present. But there is a need to recognize it is the concrete moment of a symbolic richness, which Ricoeur calls a *mixed texture*[16] whereby the opposed poles of the dialectic between archaeology and teleology are held in a hermeneutical movement. That is, the symbolic richness, or overdetermination in Freudian analysis,[17] that makes possible the process of interpretation from concealment to disclosure, from suspicion to affirmation, is contained in the *concrete mixed texture* which is the symbol.

Objective Nature of Symbols

This concrete mixed texture is the effect of the convergence, the centripetal dynamic, the bringing together of the iconic moment, the symbolic characteristic, of metaphor as the expression of being-in-the-world in the context of the symbolic richness related to conscious, subconscious and corporeal activity. The iconic moment of metaphor is the grounding of rational discourse in the ontological expression of being-in-the-world.

There are three linguistic integrally related elements of the iconic moment involved in the dynamic of metaphor that effects a convergence of symbolic activity. In metaphoric expression, an expression of historic experience of being-in-the-world, there is a convergence of symbolic activity with respect to the contextual symbolic richness relating to all levels of consciousness and corporeal activity. The three linguistic elements are imagination, image and sound. The first, which is based upon Ricoeur's interpretation and development of the Kantian notion of the productive imagination[18] and is central to his whole philosophy, will be the subject of a detailed examination in Chapter 7. The important characteristic of Ricoeur's understanding of the imagination with regard to the iconic moment of metaphor is the way that language is transcended in and through language; that the dynamic of this converging moment is the imaginative act directed beyond language in and through the mediation of linguistic symbolic structuring of human activity; a symbolic richness which in this converging moment is subjected to a dialectical tension of suspicion and affirmation. The power of the productive imagination, essentially linguistic, is its creative play of images, the second element of the iconic moment. For example, Aristotle defines the creative artistry of the poet as follows,

> ...the greatest gift by far is to be the master of the metaphor. It is the one thing that cannot be learnt from others; and it is also a sign of genius, since a good metaphor implies an intuitive perception of the similarity of dissimilars.
> (*Poetics*, 1459 a, 3 & 8)

This gift of perceiving similarity of dissimilars, essentially dependent and derivative from the creative play of images, produces an iconic fusion in an image grounded in the living present.

Poetic Language: Sound and Image

The nature of this grounding is given in sound, the third element of the iconic moment (although it must be clear that imagination, image and sound are inseparable). The key to the attempt to ground expression in the living present lies with the possibility of showing that, in this sense, language has an objective materiality. This is why the voice was so important to Husserl. It is the sound of the living voice that may ground language in the present, although Derrida's criticism of Husserl has already been noted and will be taken up again in relation to Ricoeur's theory of metaphor. However, the voice as the grounding of imaginative expression in contrast to expression of rational unity is fundamentally a different approach to sound as linguistic objective materiality. The latter is an attempt to understand how the sound of the voice in the living present is bound up with the imaginative play of images in the fusion of the iconic moment.

As mentioned above, Ricoeur is influenced by his study of religious symbols in the way that liturgical sacraments are concrete symbols which are the means of active participation.[19] The sensible objective materiality of these symbols means that they are not simply signs of 'this for that' but the mediation of human activity in the living present. Liturgical symbols, as an example of the symbolic structuring of historical, social contexts, show how people actively inhabit the lifeworld of the liturgy which is ontologically structured by the material, objective presence of the symbols. The sensible materiality of the religious symbol is analogous to the sensible materiality of the linguistic symbol; that is, the sound of the living voice. It is this that grounds the mediation of the linguistic symbol, the iconic moment of metaphor, in the immediacy of the present.

Taking, as an example, a metaphor for old age, specifically, the figure of an elderly man in the poem, *Sailing to Byzantium* by W.B. Yeats,

> An aged man is but a paltry thing
> A tattered coat upon a stick ...

The image of the old man as a tattered coat upon a stick is the result of Yeats's working with images. It is the power of the imagination to create intuitively an image through a process of fusion of images drawn from the linguistic symbolic structuring of consciousness at all levels. This is a process of image-making analogous to any artistic creativity. This linguistic process of working with words is radically different from the working out of a propositional, descriptive sentence. For example, the possible paraphrases of the above metaphor, (such as, an aged man is frail and insignificant) are 'objective descriptions' of an old man. To use Saussurean language, they are signifiers based upon an internal differential system of meaning whereby they signify the signified.[20] This is working with words in the attempt to describe the figure of an aged man through signification, that is, working with words as signs. This is not what the poet does. Neither is this the process in the creation of metaphor. Ricoeur writes,

> The poet, in effect, is that artisan who sustains and shapes imagery using no other means than language.
> (*The Rule of Metaphor*, p. 211)

What does this mean? It means that a poet like Yeats is predominantly working with sound, with rhythm, with those acoustic modulations which are the very stuff of linguistic imagery. It is immediate sensibility that is the basic means of the linguistic image making. In the same way as the sculptor's image is created out of the marble, that the materiality of the marble, its texture, its particular makeup is fundamental in the fusion of the image, so too phonic sensibility is the warp and weave of metaphor.

Reading poetry is an act of listening and seeing as the grounding of mediation of understanding. To listen to the sounds of the words,

> The yellow fog that rubs its back upon the window panes,
> (*The Love Song of J.Alfred Prufrock*, T.S. Eliot)

or,

> Pale Flakes with fingering stealth come feeling our faces –
> (*Exposure*, Wilfred Owen)

is to be responsive to the arousal of images that fuse into a configuration which makes disclosure possible in provoking semantic interaction at the level of reflection.

In his work on narrative, Ricoeur attempts to show that its composition is anchored in the symbolic resources of the practical field. That is, all actions are symbolically mediated, and therefore symbols are interpretants of action: 'Symbolism confers an initial readability on action.'[21] The linguistic trace is woven into the texture of the symbolic system of social activity. 'The tattered coat and stick' is not simply drawn from language describing utilitarian items of clothing and aids for disability; it symbolizes an active condition of particular people recognizable in the social context. Every aspect and activity of social life is potentially or actually part of its symbolic texture. It is through metaphor that symbols, in terms of image and sound, are part of language and ground linguistic mediation in the ontological condition of being-in-the-world.

The fundamental feature of this process is the way that the symbolic image is united with sound. It is important to listen to the sound when reading metaphor (whether reading aloud, or listening with the 'inner ear'). It is that sound in relation to meaning which is decisive in the choice of metaphor in the process of drawing upon background, symbolically structured social activity. This is why the creative ability required for translation involves the intuitive grasp of sound and image in both languages. Metaphor cannot be translated in the manner of seeking equivalent lexical meaning, but by an imaginative, intuitive perception rooted in sound and image of both languages.[22] The process of listening in the creation of metaphor, or an appropriation of sound in reading, is not limited to the phonics of lexical meaning based upon the notion of Saussurean *difference*; that is, sound related to linguistic concepts, which can be, according to Derrida, relinquished in favour of inscription,[23] so that sound is not the basis of meaning but writing whereby meaning is endlessly deferred through the process of metaphor, or, more particularly, metonymy.[24] In contrast, the phonics of metaphor is essential to the dynamic of the centripetal fusion of images in the intuitive perception of similarity between dissimilars. Of course, the semantics of metaphor is what matters in the affirmation of presence, but what I am claiming is that this cannot be separated from sound. In this sense, there is an agreement with Husserl that the voice is involved in the affirmation of presence, although not as the expression of the transcendental subject and the grounding of univocity.

Image, Sound and Objectivity

There is a question, however, as to whether the image can be placed on the side of objectivity, or must it inevitably be defined as a mental image and placed clearly on the subjective side? If the affirmation of presence is to be grounded in the given of linguistically structured consciousness, and not in the metaphysical assumptions of the transcendental subject, and if metaphor plays a crucial role in this grounding, then should not the image, or imaginality, be on the side of objectivity?

Husserl is concerned is to separate the image from intentionality in order to ground the intuitive unity of the object upon the latter. According to Husserl, the image-theory poses the appearance of the image in consciousness as the representative (*im bildlichen Vorstellen*) of the object. The image is the resemblance of the object in experience, but such resemblance cannot provide access to the original beyond the image. On the basis of this theory, it is not possible therefore for intentionality, for meaning, to be directed at the object. What constitutes the image as a representation of the object is intentional consciousness. Husserl's notion of intentionality is not a matter of a relation between two things: an act and an intentional object in consciousness, but one intentional experience by which the object appears. As John Sallis writes,

Husserl refers, finally, back to the domain of fundamental problems, to what is preeminently at issue in that domain, namely intentionality. It is imperative to realize that an object is present to consciousness, not because a content similar to the object is somehow present in consciousness, but rather because it is constituted as object in and through the intentional experience.
(*Delimitations*, p. 67)

Sallis takes up this critical problem in his study, in chapter 5, 'Image and Phenomena', particularly the subsection 'Image and Imaginality'. He observes that Husserl's critical achievement in insisting on the distinction between intentional experience and the intentional object, which has the effect of removing the latter from the sphere of immanence, serves to eliminate the mental object, clears the way for a return to the thing-itself, as it shows itself. The issue therefore is, if it is part of the fundamental problem of presence, how may the image be regarded as belonging to the domain of the object? According to Sallis, in his phenomenological analysis,[25] Husserl does not allow the image to be the basis of presentation because it is constituted by intentional experience. The intentional object, which Husserl identifies as the actual object, the original, appears, is presented as an image that is constituted by intentionality. For the image to participate in the process of presentation, it would have to be involved in objectivity. That is, intentional experience would have to be in relation to the image as object; its imaginality would have to be made manifest. Husserl claims that this cannot be because the image is not a predicate of the object.

My concern is not to claim that the image provides access to the thing-itself in terms of rational unity, but that it opens up the possibility of affirming such unity on the basis of ontological unity with respect to self-identity. The image is the expression of being-in-the-world. Its objectivity lies in the integral relationship with linguistic materiality of sound, the living voice, in the iconic moment of metaphor. Furthermore, intentionality, is fundamentally, with respect to the creation of meaning in a hermeneutical process, an imaginative act. It is an ontological act of expression; an imaginative expression of being-in-the-world. This act is a creative process whereby intentionality is understood as working with linguistic images. Ricoeur writes,

In poetic language, the sign is looked at, not through. In other words, instead of being a medium or route crossed on the way to reality, language itself becomes 'stuff,' like the sculptor's marble.
(*The Rule of Metaphor*, p. 209)

The ontological unity through linguistic expression in the poetic mode is achieved on the basis of an objective linguistic operation in terms of an imaginative act which fuses the linguistic images of similarity in dissimilarity in the iconic moment.

Metaphor and Rational Unity: the Interactive Theory

What then is the relationship between this act and the first critical perspective regarding the affirmation of rational unity? To put it another way, how does the imaginative act enable the 'route to be crossed on the way to reality'? Or can it? If there is not some way whereby language may refer to the reality of the thing-itself, is not conceptual unity a pragmatic or conventional achievement, for example, based upon 'use' in a Wittgensteinian 'language-game'? Or is conceptual unity an illusion; is it endlessly deferred, as Derrida claims, which will be considered briefly below?

My aim is to address this question by pursuing the semantic characteristic of Ricoeur's interactive theory of metaphor. A critical feature of this theory is that although the iconic moment is the sensible figurative focus that precipitates the *metaphora*[26] of the meaning in the semantic order, it is distinctly separate from this order. It is the linguistic dynamic of a semantic interaction process, but its sensible qualities are of a different order. The contrast with the traditional substitutional theory of metaphor reveals the key significance of this critical feature. The traditional theory is based upon metaphor as the word. Although there are many variations of this theory, particularly in the increased interest that has been recently given to the study of metaphor,[27] the critical characteristic is the 'carrying over' of one word in an act of substituting a word having a literal meaning, or a descriptive phrase with a word which conveys the effect of surprise and/or heightened emotion. The aim is to 'animate' the text for poetic or rhetorical effects. The word becomes a linguistic instrument for emotional effect. Its semantic property does not create new meaning in being 'carried over'; its deviance or impertinence is simply to bring about an intensity of perception and feeling. In the powerful first chapter of Thomas Hardy's *Return of the Native*, in describing Egdon Heath, Hardy writes,

> Haggard Egdon appealed to a subtler and scarcer instinct, to a more recently learnt emotion, than that which responds to the sort of beauty called charming and fair. (p. 34)

The literal meaning of 'Haggard' is related to a human being, or possibly an animal, which is wild-looking, especially resulting from fatigue (*OED*). Therefore it cannot be applied literally to an area of land such as a heath. The effect of its literal meaning therefore, according to the substitutional theory, is to stimulate an emotional response to the heath. The meaning of heath does not change; it remains a waste tract of land, but the feeling for this particular heath in the story is intensified.

In contrast, the interactive theory of metaphor is not based upon the word but the sentence or discourse. Metaphor understood as a process, *metaphora*, is not limited to the single word, it is the whole sentence or text. In Study 1, 'Between rhetoric and poetics: Aristotle' of *The Rule of Metaphor*, Ricoeur identifies the first characteristic of metaphor as 'something that happens to the noun' (p. 16), but claims that this became definitive of the dominant view confining metaphor to one of the figures of speech contained in Aristotle's theory of tropes. This view, resulting, according to Ricoeur, from a decline in the importance of rhetoric and a separation between speculative and poetic discourse,[28] led to a failure to recognize the fundamental importance of the second characteristic. He writes,

> The second characteristic is that *metaphor is defined in terms of movement*. The *epiphora* of a word is described as a sort of displacement, a movement 'from … to … ' This notion of *epiphora* enlightens at the same time as it puzzles us. It tells us that, far from designating just one figure of speech among others such as synecdoche and metonymy (this is how we find metaphor taxonomized in later rhetoric), for Aristotle the word *metaphor* applies to every transposition of terms. (*Ibid.*, p. 17)

This movement is later developed in his analysis to be understood in philosophical terms as the ontological dynamic of convergence in the iconic moment of metaphor. Here it can be seen to relate to the semantic movement with respect to metaphor defined in terms of the sentence or the complete discourse. In other words, what happens in the movement of metaphor is a displacement of meaning in a process of semantic interaction between what may be described as semantic fields.[29] In the above example, the word 'haggard' carries over the semantic connotations from the field of its literal meaning to interact with the semantic field of the noun, 'heath'. The *epiphoric* semantic convergence of these two fields is brought about by the fusion of images in the iconic moment.

Metaphor: Split Reference

Ricoeur describes this as an ontological vehemence which uproots the literal reference in one field to set free a second-order, metaphorical reference to interact in another semantic. Here, he draws upon the literary criticism in the work of Roman Jacobson, particularly his notion of *split reference*.[30] He writes,

> The most radical consequences of this is that what happens in poetry is not the suppression of referential function but its profound alteration by the working of ambiguity: 'The supremacy of poetic function over referential function does not obliterate the reference but makes it ambiguous. The double-sensed message finds its correspondence in a split addresser, in a split addressee, and what is more in a split reference, as is cogently exposed in the preambles to fairy tales of various peoples, for instance, in the usual exordium of the Majorca storytellers: 'Aixo era y no era' (It was and it was not)'
> (*Ibid.*, p. 224)

What Ricoeur is at pains to make clear is reference, in this sense of metaphorical second-order reference, is not the literal denotation of rational identity, but the reference to an active state of affairs, to a lifeworld appropriated and inhabited by an act of the imagination that is linguistic through and through. With regard to metaphor, it is through the iconic moment that this reference is made possible; but to consider the full implications of this notion of split reference in relation to the imaginative act will require the critical analysis of Ricoeur's theory of narrative set out in the next chapter. The issue at this stage is how is conceptual unity achieved at the semantic level in affirming the presence of the thing-itself? If the interactive process is based upon ambiguity, and involves reference which is of second-order association and connotation, not literal denotation, how is it possible for conceptual unity to be achieved?

Two Levels of Operation: Figurative and Semantic

The interactive theory of metaphor is based upon an understanding of metaphor as sentence or discourse not a single word. The sentence, the basic unit of language refers to the reality of the objective world because meaning is based upon this unit. Words only have meaning in relation to the sentences or discourse of which they are part. With the exception of proper names which are limited to designation, all lexical definitions are interpreted by reference to other words on the basis of the sentence or discourse. The literal abstract meaning is created out of a dialectic between the two levels of operation: the metaphorical operation whereby reference is achieved through the sentence, and the level of abstract meaning with respect to rational discourse based upon the word. In defining this dialectic, Ricoeur presents his particular interpretation of what Hegel calls *Aufhebung*.[31] In Study Eight of *The Rule of Metaphor*, he writes:

> The first operation which is purely metaphorical, takes a proper (*eigentlich*) meaning and transports it (*übertragen*) into the spiritual order. Out of expression – non-proper (*uneigentlich*) because transposed – the other operation makes a proper abstract meaning. It is the second operation that constitutes the 'suppression-preservation' which Hegel calls *Aufhebung*. But the two operations, transfer *and* suppression-preservation, are distinct. The second alone creates a proper sense in the spiritual order out of an improper sense coming from the sensible order. The phenomenon of wearing away (*Abnutzung*) is only a prior condition allowing the second operation to be constituted on the ground of the first.
> (*Ibid.*, p. 292)

Conceptuality in speculative, rational discourse is constituted on the ground of the metaphoric iconic focus in a primordial dialectical relationship whereby the interactive process of the semantic fields brings about the creation of new meaning. As the sensible element wears away through continuing use over time, the proper sense of the new meaning is constituted in the rational, conceptual order.

But the question remains, how can conceptual unity be constituted on the basis of ambiguity in the metaphorical order? Janet Martin Soskice writes,

> In *The Rule of Metaphor*, Paul Ricoeur comes perilously close to committing himself to both a 'dual sense' and a 'dual truth' thesis. Metaphor and Religious Language.
> (*Metaphor and Religious Language*, p. 86)

She is critical of Ricoeur's attempt to appropriate the Hegelian notion of *Aufhebung*. Ricoeur claims that through the ontological vehemence of the iconic moment a tension is set up 'deep within the logical force of the verb *to be*' between an impossibility of a literal interpretation and the metaphorical 'is'. That is, the tension between the 'is' and the 'is not'. He writes, with respect to the metaphorical 'is',

> To state 'that is' – such is the moment of *belief*, of *ontological commitment*, which gives affirmation its 'illocutionary' force.
> (*Ibid.*, p. 249)

Here Ricoeur is drawing upon the Speech Act theories of J.L. Austin and John Searle in which language is understood to be performative in the sense that certain forms of speech are central to the performance of the acts that are expressed. An aim of this study is to draw upon Ricoeur's dynamic theory of metaphor in an attempt to show how unity, in terms of the iconic moment achieved through an active, ontological commitment, makes possible conceptual unity within the tension set up in semantic interaction between the 'is' and the 'is not'.

As a result, new meaning is created whereby there is a redescription. Through the power of metaphor, the active lifeworld which is symbolically and linguistically structured is constantly redescribed making possible logical, rational analysis and explanation in relation to the entities abstracted from the lifeworld. Metaphorical, poetic language is 'fluid' open to the expansiveness of the experience of the lifeworld, constantly disclosing the new meanings of the opaque richness of the symbolic structure and sedimentation at all levels of consciousness in a hermeneutical process from suspicion to affirmation.

Soskice's criticism of this theory of metaphor, in which she takes note of the work of Max Black which influenced Ricoeur, deserves quoting at length.

> Ricoeur's suggestion that the tension of metaphor is ontological is somewhat ambiguous. It is motivated in part by his desire to emphasize the redescriptive power of metaphor, hence the 'critical incision of the (literal) "is not" within the ontological vehemence of the (metaphorical) "is"' The most obvious reading of these remarks about redescription and ontological tension is as a restatement of

theunsatisfactory (A is a B) 'two-subjects' view that we have criticized in Max Black, thus 'Man is a wolf' and 'Man is not a wolf', 'The lake is sapphire' and 'The lake is not sapphire'. ... But this approach comes dangerously near to making metaphor a matter of comparison and Ricoeur's use of the term 'redescription' is revealing. The trouble with Black's theory is that, in assuming a two-subject perspective in which primary subject (man) is modified by the secondary subject (wolf), he is unable to explain convincingly how metaphors can say something genuinely new. Similarly Ricoeur's language of redescription inevitably suggests comparison because, even accompanied by talk of an ontological tension, it implies that there is some definite, pre-existing thing (the principal subject of the metaphor in Max Black's terms) that the metaphor is *about* and simply redescribes. (*Ibid.*, p. 89)

This criticism seems to be unanswerable within the confines of Ricoeur's theory set out in *The Rule of Metaphor*. It is only in the development of Ricoeur's work in his theory of narrative, and particularly narrative identity that the critical issue may be addressed. What is at stake is not a pre-existing principal subject, but the teleological movement from suspicion to affirmation of self-identity grounded in ontological commitment mediated through the text, in terms of narrative identity, that is the dynamic of new meaning, and not of comparison.

Derridean Perspective: Critical Questions

In this chapter I have raised fundamental questions with respect to Ricoeur's two critical perspectives upon the problem of presence. These may be clear from the comparison with Derrida. Although both are committed to the givenness of a phenomenological perspective on language as the basis of any attempt to address the problem of presence, and, consequently, to exclude all metaphysical assumptions, Derrida's understanding of metaphor may seem to remain faithful to this commitment in contrast to Ricoeur. Derrida takes the linguistic sign system in terms of inscription, since sound, the living voice, he attempts to show, assumes the presence of a transcendental subject, and therefore an *a priori* metaphysical foundation for presence. Accordingly, he is committed to inscription, the mark, the linguistic trace as the basis of any approach to the problem of presence. Any question of the derivation of meaning is confined to *l'écriture*. Meaning is the effect of the play, the dissemination of this trace in terms of Saussurean difference, but inscriptive not phonic.[32] Metaphor is the nature of this play. It is the semantic movement in the context of continually changing experience; a constant reverberation in which there is a process of supplementing the *space* in the *trace*. Metaphor, therefore, is this movement of supplementarity in an endless metonymic chain, a process in which meaning is never achieved but endlessly deferred; which is the reason for Derrida coining the word *Différance* to combine the notions of difference and deferred. Derrida makes clear that the trace, in terms of this endless metaphoric supplementarity whereby presence cannot be affirmed, determines consciousness; and intentionality, intuition and the imagination are linguistically derivative with respect to the trace.

My intention in this brief reference to Derrida's understanding of metaphor is to indicate a fundamental distinction between Derrida and Ricoeur which provides a critical perspective on the latter's commitment to the givenness of the text; secondly, to make note of a critical contrasting view which will remain central to this study and be taken up at a later stage. With respect to the first critical perspective of the problem of affirming rational unity, Ricoeur's response in terms of his theory of metaphor raises the question, what kind of unity is mediated through the poetic mode of language as the grounding of rational unity? What is the linguistic nature of ontological vehemence and tension in the iconic moment which achieves a fusion based upon an ambiguity that is never completely transcended? Or, in other words, an ambiguity between suspicion and affirmation with the movement towards the latter but never relinquishing suspicion? Secondly, in attempting to resolve the second critical perspective of the issue of being-in-the-world in relation to the problem, has Ricoeur gone beyond the givenness of language in the imaginative expression of the poetic mode? Does not the imagination presume a transcendental subject in a similar manner to that of Husserl? Does not the sound of the living voice, even in the poetic mode, point to the extra linguistic presence of the transcendental subject? How is it possible for the imagination to be linguistic and yet transcend language in referring to the objective lifeworld? To take up these questions it is necessary to follow the development of Ricoeur's work on metaphor in his theory of narrative.

Notes

1. *The Symbolism of Evil* is part of the early trilogy, including *Fallible Man* and *Freedom and Nature: The Voluntary and the Involuntary*, in which he first addresses the nature of the symbolic with respect to concrete expressions of the human experience of evil. His aim is to identify a method for making sense of mythic language which is symbolic through and through. Later, he developed this work on the symbolic features of metaphor and narrative. See *Time and Narrative*, Vol i, pp. 57–8.
2. In *Creative Evolution*, chapter 1, Bergson writes, 'Time is an invention or it is nothing at all.' He explains that creative time or *duration* is originally experienced as time lived in the stream of consciousness and then applied by analogy to the universe. Therefore it is inner time that is being analysed. From Bergson's view, calendar time is merely an externalized form of time, a 'fall' of time in the direction of spatialization.
3. It is 'non-conceptual' in the paradoxical sense that, according to Heidegger, cannot be defined in terms of traditional Western logic. See Introduction, Part I, *Being and Time*. For a discussion of this paradox in the context of a penetrating account of the problem of Being, see *An Introduction to Metaphysics*.

4. See *Narrative in Culture*, ed. Cristopher Nash; also *Love's Knowledge*, Martha C. Nussbaum.

5. See Study 1 in *The Rule of Metaphor*. In his *Poetics*, Aristotle sets out his definition of metaphor as 'the application of an alien name by a transference either from genus to species, or from species to genus, or from species to species, or by analogy', 1457b 4–9. He also discusses the use of metaphor with respect to style in section 9 of the *Rhetoric*.

6. In *The Philosophy of Rhetoric*, I.A. Richards was the first to propose that two ideas are active together in metaphor, although he did not offer any explicit definition or theory. Nevertheless, he did identify the one idea as the *vehicle* which is conveyed by the literal meaning of the words used metaphorically, and the *tenor* as the idea conveyed by the *vehicle*. The metaphor is neither the *vehicle* nor the *tenor* but the two conjoined.

7. In *Models and Metaphors*, Max Black makes a number of significant contributions and emendations to Richards. He claims that a metaphor is not an isolated term but a sentence. He calls the metaphorical sentence the *frame*, and the word or words used the *focus*.

8. To account for metaphorical meaning, Monroe C. Beardsley, in his *Aesthetics*, makes a distinction between designation, denotation and connotation. In a metaphor there appears a falsehood or logical absurdity that makes reading at the level of designation of the terms impossible. Consequently, the reader falls back on the level of connotation that is called metaphor. In Beardsley's 'controversion' theory, as it is called, there is a conflict of word meaning in metaphor that is resolved by moving down the hierarchy of readings.

9. The 'ornamental' or 'emotional' theory of metaphor has been dominant in the traditional theories until this century, although, Ricoeur, among others, attempts to show the historical roots of these theories in Aristotle's *Poetics* and *Rhetoric*. See Study 1, *The Rule of Metaphor*. See also 'The Classical View' in Terence Hawkes' *Metaphor*; and 'Classical Accounts of Metaphor' in Janet Martin Soskice's *Metaphor and Religious Language*. The key issue is whether metaphor has a cognitive element, or is simply an emotional figure of speech.

10. See *The Rule of Metaphor*, p. 313.

11. *Ibid.*, pp. 299–30.

12. *Ibid.*, pp. 187–91.

13. The notion of *lebenswelt*, or lifeworld, first introduced into hermeneutical philosophy by Wilhelm Dilthey (see 'The Construction of the Historic World in Human Studies', *Dilthey's Selected Writings*).

14. Ricoeur's notion of the 'hermeneutics of suspicion' became clearer in his thought during his work on Freud. At the end of this study, in establishing a dialectic between suspicion and faith, drawing upon Merleau-Ponty's term for psychoanalysis, the 'archaeology of the subject' as the topography for the unmasking of illusions, he proposes that, faith being the opposite of suspicion, there must be a 'teleology of the subject'. Consequently, he creates a dialectic between psychoanalysis as the interpretation of the unconscious and eschatological hope which moves beyond a human being is to what he may become. See *Freud and Philosophy*, Book III, Chapters 2 and 3.

15. Ricoeur's interest in Paul Tillich's view on symbols was influential in the development of his thought. See Tillich's essay, 'The Religious Symbol' in a collection of essays under the title *Myth and Symbol*, ed. F.W. Dillistone, and

John E. Smith's essay, 'Freud, Philosophy and Interpretation' in *The Philosophy of Paul Ricoeur*, ed. Lewis E. Hahn, pp. 150–52.

16. *Freud and Philosophy*, p. 494.
17. *Freud and Philosophy*, pp. 93–5 and 496–506.
18. Kant, *Critique of Judgment*, §314.
19. Among others, Paul Tillich's theological interpretation of social and religious symbols with respect to an immanent participation in a transcendent ultimate reality (e.g. Part 2, 'Concrete Applications' *in Theology of Culture*, and the work of Ernst Cassirer, *The Philosophy of Symbolic Forms*) was profoundly influential in the development of Ricoeur's thought, leading to the description of the symbolic resources of the practical field as the second anchorage of *Mimêsis1* in *Time and Narrative*, vol. 1, pp. 57–8. See also Northrop Frye's essay, 'Theory of Symbols' in *Anatomy of Criticism*.
20. See note 27, Chapter 1.
21. *Time and Narrative*, Vol. 1, p. 58.
22. Translation must take account of sound considering its fundamental significance with respect to the historical developments of any particular language (see 'The Importance of Sound-changes' in *A History of the English Language*, Albert C. Baugh and Thomas Cable pp. 230–35). However, the theory that language has its roots in metaphor and narrative means that this particular historical development of sound-change is grounded in the rhythmic sound patterns and images of a linguistic culture or lifeworld. Translation therefore involves an appropriation of a linguistic lifeworld of which sound and image of metaphor are primary.
23. Derrida writes, 'The primitive meaning, the original, and always sensual and material figure . ..is not exactly a metaphor. It is a kind of transparent figure, equivalent to a literal meaning (*sens propre*). It becomes a metaphor when philosophical discourse puts it into circulation. Simultaneously the first meaning and first displacement are forgotten. The metaphor is no longer noticed, and it is taken for the proper meaning' ('White Mythology' in *Margins of Philosophy*, p. 211). This proper meaning, however, according to Derrida, is an illusion. Language is subject to *Différance*, the endless play of metaphoric displacement, which he describes in terms of 'supplementarity' and 'spacing'; a play of language as a system of inscribed signs, of writing or *l'écriture*.
24. Derrida's understanding of metaphor in a metonymic sense closely relates to the question of western metaphysics and presence, and the withdrawal of Being. He writes, 'This metaphysics *as* a tropical system and singularly as a metaphoric detour would correspond to the *withdrawal* of Being: unable to reveal itself except in dissimulating itself under the 'species' of an epochal determination, under the species of an *as* which obliterates itself *as such* (Being *as* eidos, *as* subjectity, *as* will, *as* work, etc.), Being would allow itself to be named in a metaphorico-metonymical divergence (*écart*). One would then be tempted to say: the metaphysical, which corresponds in its discourse to the withdrawal of Being, tends to reassemble, in resemblance, all its metonymic divergences in a great metaphor of Being or of the thought of Being. This bringing together is *the* language of metaphysics *itself*.' 'The Retrait of Metaphor', p. 21.
25. *Delimitations*, John Sallis, pp. 67–8.
26. In chapter 21 of the *Poetics*, Aristotle follows the derivation of the term 'metaphor' in saying that *metaphora* (carrying across) is a kind of *epiphora* (carrying over). The 'carrying over', or transference is a word, or word's meaning.

In the traditional theory of 'carrying over' it is for the purpose of substituting one word for another. The word's meaning stimulates surprise and emotion by the nature of its deviance. The 'carrying over' is not a cognitive process, and does not involve any change or creation of meaning. According to this theory, metaphor is one type of trope in the classical glossary of figures of speech. According to Ricoeur (*Rule of Metaphor*, Study 1, p. 17), for Aristotle's definition of *metaphora* a sort of displacement applies to every transposition of terms. He claims that this understanding of transpositional movement may be seen to apply to all domains including the sentence, and therefore it is movement involving semantic change.

27. Nietzsche's view of metaphor has had profound effects on Derrida and many 'postmodernist' philosophers. See *Nietzsche and Metaphor*, Sarah Kofman.

28. See Study 2 in *The Rule of Metaphor*. For the renewed interest in the contemporary developments of literary studies and philosophy, see *The Bible as Rhetoric*, ed. Martin Warner; also, *Persuasion: Greek Rhetoric in Action*, ed. Ian Worthington.

29. See Eva Feder Kittay, 'Semantic Field Theory', chapter 6, *Metaphor*.

30. See *Rule of Metaphor*, pp. 222–28.

31. The Hegelian term *aufhebung* has still not been really translated, or rethought in English. See an additional note of Hegel's *The Encyclopaedia Logic*, trans. T.F. Geraets, W.A. Suchting, and H.S. Harris, '...we should remember the double meaning of the German expression "*aufheben*". On the one hand, we understand it to mean "clear away" or "cancel", and in that sense we say a law or regulation is cancelled (*aufgehoben*). But the word "to preserve", and we say in this sense that something is well taken care of (*wohl aufgehoben*). This ambiguity in linguistic usage, through which the same word has a negative and a positive meaning, cannot be regarded as an accident nor yet as a reason to reproach language as if it were a source of confusion. We ought rather to recognise here the speculative spirit of our language which transcends the "either-or" of mere understanding.' p. 154. In the contemporary Continental philosophic debate there are a number of varied interpretations of this concept. Derrida says, 'We will never be finished with the reading or re-reading of Hegel, and in a certain way, I do nothing other than attempt to explain myself on this point.' Quoted in the Introduction to *Hegel After Derrida*, ed. Stuart Barners, p. 1. In the essay by Kevin Thompson, 'Hegelian Dialectic and the Quasi-Transcendental in Glas' he claims that there is a deep affinity between *aufhebung* and *différance*. p. 239.

32. See Ferdinand de Saussure's *Course in General Linguistics*, tr. Roy Harris [23ff], p. 8ff.

Chapter 3

Metaphor and Narrative

Narrative and the Questions of Presence

The questions raised at the conclusion of Chapter 2 with respect to the critical perspectives identified in Chapter 1 draw attention to the unresolved problem of presence. Metaphor is the critical linguistic focus for achieving this resolution; but in order carefully to consider whether this resolution is possible, it is necessary to pursue the analysis of metaphor with respect to narrative, drawing upon Ricoeur's theory set out in *Time and Narrative* and *Oneself as Another*.

The reason for developing the analysis of metaphor in this direction is to concentrate upon the issues relating to the poetic mode of language as the linguistic mediation for the grounding and affirming of presence – the mode of language which may be understood as the ontological expression of being-in-the-world. The essential characteristic of this mode is the symbolic grounding of its figuration in the concrete activity of the lifeworld. There are two key questions arising from Ricoeur's theory of metaphor: first, what kind of unity is achieved through this grounding in the iconic moment whereby the poetic mode dynamically affirms conceptual unity in the rational mode of language? How is it possible for univocity, and therefore presence of objects, to be affirmed by means of the mediation of a linguistic mode that seems to be rooted in ambiguity and contradiction? In the rational tradition of Western philosophy there has been constant vigilance in upholding the law of non-contradiction,[1] and a dominant concern to separate the rational and poetic modes of language.[2] This question relates directly to the issue of temporality which was outlined in Chapter 1 and must be given closer attention.

The second question is, how is it possible for the poetic mode of language, as defined by Ricoeur in his work on metaphor and narrative, to be transcended in and through language? What is being considered in this study is how this mode of language is the given mediation of consciousness whereby presence is affirmed by means of an intrinsic dynamic, ontologically grounded in the activity of the lifeworld, which is transcendental and teleological, and which has metaphysical implications. More particularly, this study considers the principal part played by the imagination in this process of affirmation when defined in terms of linguistic figuration and the corporeal nature of consciousness.

This chapter will be devoted more to the importance of sound with respect to the objective and ontological characteristics of metaphor and narrative, and the unity of self-identity. Therefore, it is the first question which will mainly be addressed in this and the following chapter; the question of transcendence, although being touched upon in this chapter and the next, will predominate in relation to a development of the Kantian notion of the productive imagination in Chapter 7.

Saussure and Sound

In raising the question about unity, it is critically important to understand the difference between that unity of self-identity which is achieved by the iconic moment of the poetic mode related to the figurative characteristic of metaphor and the configuration of narrative,[3] and the conceptual unity that, for example, according to Ferdinand de Saussure,[4] is phonically achieved by the internal structures of the linguistic synchronic sign system. It is in relation to the latter that Derrida criticizes Saussure, particularly in *Of Grammatology*,[5] for giving priority to sound in language, but there is a significant difference to that taken in this study. Saussure's perspective with respect to univocity is based upon the rational, conceptual mode of language, whereas my approach to unity is grounded in the poetic mode.

Saussure defines language as a sign system based upon the notion of the linguistic sign consisting of two elements. In 'The Linguistic Sign' taken from his *Course in General Linguistics* he writes,

> A linguistic sign is not a link between a thing and a name, but between a concept and a sound pattern. The sound pattern is not actually a sound; for a sound is something physical. A sound pattern is the hearer's psychological impression of a sound, as given to him by the evidence of his senses. This sound pattern may be called a 'material' element only in that it is the representation of our sensory impressions. The sound pattern may thus be distinguished from the other element associated with it in the linguistic sign. This other element is generally of a more abstract kind: the concept.
> (*Course in General Linguistics*, p. 66)

The concept he calls the *signified*, and the sound-image is the *signifier*. This latter element of the sign, according to Saussure, reveals how language is grounded in the concrete and particular, in the way the sound of the spoken word makes a psychological imprint in terms of an image which is integrally related to the former element of the sign, that is, the concept or cognitive idea. However, the sound-image, the signifier, does not refer to the object in the manner of an empirical sense-image, but to the concept, the signified as the mediation of the object. In other words, although language is grounded in the concrete and the particular in the spoken word, linguistic meaning is an internal production of the sign system. For this reason, Saussure is equally concerned to separate the sign system of language, *langue*, from the spoken word – speech, *parole* – to show how the structure of the sign system produces meaning by an internal process; the meaning of words, being based upon a purely arbitrary process with respect to phonic difference, is determined by convention. He writes,

> For any means of expression accepted in a society rests in principle upon a collective habit, or on convention, which comes to the same thing.
> (*Ibid.*, p. 68)

In the light of Saussure's definition of the arbitrary nature of linguistic meaning, particularly his view of *symbol*, and the central role played by the symbolic characteristic of metaphor as discussed in the previous chapter, it is important to appreciate the difference between these contrasting theories in which sound is fundamental to both. Saussure writes,

> The word *symbol* is sometimes used to designate the linguistic sign, or more exactly that part of the linguistic sign which we are calling the signal. This use of the word *symbol* is awkward, for reasons connected to the first principle. For it is characteristic of symbols that they are never entirely arbitrary. They are not empty configurations. They show at least a vestige of natural connexion between the signal and its signification. For instance, our symbol of justice, the scales could hardly be replaced by a chariot.
> (*Ibid.*, p. 68)

This understanding of symbol does not, however, take account of the ontological view of the metaphoric icon. According to this view, the symbolic characteristic of metaphor is not simply a 'this for that',[6] a linguistic sound-image signifying the object in terms of the mediation of the signified or concept. It is the mediation of a participation in the particular, concrete activity of the lifeworld. It is the mediation of an active, temporal state of being; and the nature of this mediation is the integral relationship of sound and image.

Saussure is concerned only with sound in relation to an arbitrary production of conceptual meaning; that is, meaning of single words. My concern is with sound as it relates to words as part of sentences and discourse. Sound is not limited to the structure of phonemes of the particular word; it is part of the expression of the sentence and discourse in terms of stress, accent, cadence, inflection and enunciation. This is particularly evident in poetry, but it is also true of all forms of narrative which give expression to lifeworlds. The spoken word gives expression to an imaginative participation in the world of the narrative. It is an expression of sound patterns integrally related to a state of being that is actively disturbed by the ontological reverberations of an imaginative appropriation of the world of the narrative.

Ontological Sonority

There is an objectivity to these sound patterns, which means that they are not simply a subjective mode of expression, and therefore may be analysed scientifically to determine their nature with respect to the materiality of the structure of the text. But, in a fundamental sense with regard to the creation of meaning, they cannot be analysed in terms of the scientific perspective of the subject–object relationship. These sound patterns are not to be defined in terms of the *thingness* or *whatness*[7] of objectivity, whether that be the objects of description included in a poem or narrative, or the materiality of sound as the linguistic characteristic of the poetic mode of the text. They are sound patterns of an ontological condition. In other words, the sound patterns set up by the iconic moment of metaphor, and the *mimetic configuration* of narrative play a central part in the ontological condition of the reader in the imaginative appropriation of the world of the text.

This is not, in Heideggerian terms, the ontic condition of objectivity, the traditional ontology of the thingness or whatness of the natural world included in the narrative descriptions. It is the ontological condition of Dasein, of being-in-the-world, which Heidegger attempts painstakingly to define in *Being and Time*, and later in *The Basic Problems of Phenomenology*. What is at stake is the being of the pre-objective world upon which subjective and objective being are founded. He writes,

> The world is not the sum total of extant entities. It is, quite generally, not extant at all. It is a determination of being-in-the-world, a moment in the structure of Dasein's mode of being. The world is something Dasein-ish, it is not extant like things but it is *da*, there-here, like the *Dasein*, the being-da [das Da-sein] which we ourselves are: that is to say, it exists. We call the mode of being that we ourselves are, of the Dasein, by the name of existence. This implies as a pure matter of terminology that the world is not extant but rather it exists, it has the Dasein's mode of being.
>
> (*The Basic Problems of Phenomenology*, p. 166)

However, aware that this interpretation of being may be assumed to be a form of subjective idealism, Heidegger proceeds to explain that the world is something that the subject projects outward from within itself, and in the thrownness of this projection other things are uncovered:

> To exist means, among other things, to cast-forth a world [Heidegger's phrase, *sich Welt vorher-werfen* suggests it is pre-thrown, pre-cast; it is an *a priori* of the *Dasein*], and in fact in such a way that with the thrownness of this projection, with the factical existence of a Dasein, extant entities are already uncovered.
>
> (*Ibid.*, p. 168)

At this point, the purpose of this brief reference to this aspect of Heidegger's work is to provide an ontological perspective for an interpretation of the sound patterns of metaphor and narrative. Further and more detailed consideration of Heideggerian ontology will be given in subsequent chapters. What is at issue here is the way sound may be understood as the critical feature of the thrownness of a *Dasein's* projection of the world. That is, with respect to a written text, the ontological condition of a reader's appropriation of a text, which is a hermeneutical process, is the projection of the world of the text whereby sound is the prime characteristic of the expression of this ontological condition. This involves the pre-thrownness or projection of *Dasein* in the projection or appropriation of the world of the text which sets up a primary dialectic between Self and Other, which will be the subject of analysis in Chapter 5. Here, the concern is with what may be called the 'ontological reverberations' set up by the appropriation of the intrinsic sound patterns of the metaphoric iconic moments and mimetic configuration of the text. In contrast to Saussure, the sound-image is not simply a psychological imprint but the consequence, or expression of an ontological condition, as was seen in Chapter 2, with respect to Ricoeur's understanding of symbol, whereby there is an imaginative active participation in the event, the *Ereignis* in Heideggerian terminology. That is, the symbolic image, the iconic moment, is the focus of particular intense moments of an active condition of being-in-the-world. The sound-patterns of metaphor and narrative, intrinsically related to the image, are the linguistic mediation of this ontological condition.

In Ricoeur's interpretation of this ontological condition there are two critically important features. Firstly, in the tenth study of *Oneself as Another* which poses the question *What Ontology in View?* he attempts to define ontology in terms of action. Secondly, in *Time and Narrative*, in which he acknowledges the phenomenological work of Maurice Merleau-Ponty with respect to the lived body and the power to act, activity is fundamental to Ricoeur's ontological view and the phenomenological effects. Taking Aristotle's treatment of the concepts of *dunamis* and *energeia* in the *Metaphysics*, he explores the question whether change can be included in the notion of being. He concludes that in the relation between power and act Aristotle allows a greater freedom in defining these notions so that the one cannot be established independently of the other. He writes,

> In this way, being as potentiality (beginning in 9.1–5) allows us to include change within being, contrary to Parmenides' prohibition, and, more precisely, to include local motion. Because potentiality is a genuine mode of being, change and motion are rightfully beings.
> (*Oneself as Another*, p. 304)

According to Ricoeur, the problem in Western philosophy has been in equating *energeia* with the Latin translation, *actualis*, denoting 'that in which we exist',[8] with the dominant emphasis being placed upon facticity. Does this not, he asks, 'diminish the dimension of *energeia* and of *dunamis* by virtue of which human *acting* and *suffering* are rooted in being?' It is in the maintenance of the dialectic between these two terms that there is the possibility of interpreting human action and being together as both act and potentiality.

Furthermore, this ontological view of human action may be seen to take into account the consequential effects in the phenomenology of the flesh, the lived body. It is the lived body which incarnates potentiality in the power to act of the 'I can' and action. Ricoeur writes,

> The most radical position in this respect is that by which Merleau-Ponty characterized the insertion of the acting subject in the world, namely, the experience of the 'I can', the root of the 'I am'.
> (*Time and Narrative*, Vol 3, p. 230)

But there is an ambiguity in the self's relation to the flesh in that it is both 'mine' and 'other'. And so, in this sense, the lived body is the original mediator between the course of lived experience in the world. It mediates the event in terms of human activity. This mediation engages the corporeality of the lived body in which sound is a key element. Merleau-Ponty writes,

> I am a sonorous being, but I hear my own vibration from within; as Malraux said, I hear myself with my throat. In this, as he also has said, I am incomparable; my voice is bound to the mass of my own life as is the voice of no one else.
> (*The Visible and the Invisible*, p. 144)

Relating this to the written text in the poetic mode, the appropriation of the objective text fundamentally involves the projection of the world of the text by a *Dasein*, which means that reading, understood as a hermeneutical process based upon understanding, *Verstehen*, is rooted in the thrownness of a Sonorous Being.[9] Although reading aloud may therefore be considered to be the most appropriate means for poetry and narrative, and indeed this may well be so with respect to the former,[10] the ontological reverberations set up by the intrinsic sound patterns of the written text may be seen to be the effect of the imaginative act of appropriation involving a sense of corporeal sonority.

The imaginative act is fundamentally the key to the thrownness of a *Dasein* understood as a Sonorous Being whereby the mediation of historical activity is made through corporeal sonority which is intrinsically related to phenomenological figuration at the various levels of consciousness. I will look at this with respect to corporeal figuration in the various forms including music and dance, but specifically in the particular and peculiar relationship between this imaginative act of figuration and the act of cognition – that is, between understanding and explanation, between metaphor and concept, between narrative and rational discourse. My present aim is to analyse the sound patterns of this imaginative act as the ontological dynamic of a unifying process manifested in corporeal perception founded upon an integral relationship of sound and image. In other words, the sound patterns of this ontological centripetal dynamic are intrinsically related to an act of configuration in the 'grasping'[11] of the text of the narrative.

In response to Derrida's criticism regarding the extralinguistic source of unity, the crucial question is whether the subject is the foundation of the imaginative act, or whether the text is the source of these sound patterns and figuration as the dynamic of unity? This question may be posed in terms of unity of self-identity. If the affirmation of the unity of rational discourse is founded upon the unity of self-identity, and the latter is affirmed through the mediation of the poetic mode of discourse which is appropriated by an imaginative act, from whence comes this unity of self-identity? The response to this question is in terms of what Ricoeur calls narrative identity. The source of this unity is the text; which means the text has an extralinguistic dimension, but is itself the source of this teleological dynamic of unity referring to the world beyond.

Narrative and Ontological Sonority

The remainder of this chapter is devoted to an analysis of the first part of Ricoeur's theory of narrative, and to show that it is ontological sonority which is the key to its grounding. It is this which may be seen to provide the foundation of the development of the theory, and especially narrative identity. At this juncture, it is worthwhile referring briefly again to Ricoeur's early development of his philosophical anthropology based upon existential concerns, particularly in *Fallible Man*,[12] which he calls the '*Pathetique* of "Misery" and Pure Reflection'. According to Ricoeur, the pathos of the soul is in the movement from the sensible toward the intelligible, and the perplexity, the aporia in this quest for understanding and knowledge. From Kant he borrows the threefold structure of "finite", "infinite" and the mediation between the two.[13] The progression of the soul is caught in the tension between the finite and the infinite, between the inner intuitive sense and the outer senses of consciousness. This will be elaborated further in Chapter 5 with respect to the relationship of Self and Other. It is mentioned here because in defining the nature of this tension of the soul, Ricoeur introduces the concept of 'fault' and fallibility. He writes,

> The idea that man is by nature fragile and liable to err is, according to my working hypothesis, an idea wholly accessible to pure reflection; it designates a characteristic of man's being.
> (*Fallible Man*, p. 3)

Fallibility of human nature is, therefore, ontologically, a key characteristic of a *Dasein* which may be defined in terms of sonority, a sonority which is the teleological dynamic of understanding and rational explanation; that is, the dynamic to resolve the condition of fallibility in the tension between the finite and the infinite which is manifested phenomenologically and linguistically in the creation and re-creation of meaning in a hermeneutical movement from suspicion to affirmation.

Although my concern is to consider critically Ricoeur's view that the text is the source of univocity, and therefore the mediation whereby the ontological dynamic of Sonorous Being is given a teleological dimension in the creation and re-creation of meaning, it is necessary to understand that this dynamic roots language in the various ontological and phenomenological levels of human experience and activity – for example, in the way human, historical activity is symbolized. In Ricoeur's theory of narrative, set out in *Time and Narrative*, he defines three moments of *Mimesis* in terms of figuration as the mediation of temporal human activity.[14] Developing his understanding of the Aristotelian notion of emplotment[15] with respect to the figuration of the world of human time and action, *Mimesis* is defined as the anchorage of narrative composition in the prefiguration of the practical field in its symbolic resources. In other words, temporal activity is always mediated by a kaleidoscopic structure of cultural symbols. In this respect, Ricoeur acknowledges the work of Ernst Cassirer[16] as close to his own:

> ... I have opted for one close to that of Cassirer, in his *Philosophy of Symbolic Forms*, inasmuch as, for him, symbolic forms are cultural processes that articulate experience.
> (*Time and Narrative*, Vol. 1, p. 57)

His theory of symbol has already been sketched in Chapter 2 in relation to the iconic moment of metaphor. In particular, it was seen that the symbol has a mediating function by means of active participation. Cultural symbols may therefore be understood as the structuring of the *Lebenswelt*; the ontological, corporate activity of being-in-the-world, and a patterned sonority of temporal human activity. In other words, cultural symbols are the pre-thrownness of a corporate, or intersubjective being-in-the-world. Therefore, the act of narrative composition, or the act of reading, the appropriation of the world of the narrative, are based upon an ontological thrownness or projection of a *Dasein* which resonates with its pre-thrownness. That is, the figuration of the text is rooted in cultural symbolic structuring which sets up a new pattern of sonority in the act of composition or reading.

Temporality

An important aspect of this symbolic structuring of the pre-thrownness of being-in-the-world is a pre-understanding of action; and a fundamental feature of this pre-understanding is the recognition that in action there are temporal structures which call for narration. That is, in the symbolic structuring of human activity, which may be discerned in every aspect of the

Lebenswelt, there is the condition of ontological sonority phenomenologically manifested by the power of the imagination in the mediation of patterned sound and figuration. Consequently, the vulgar speech of the *Lebenswelt* is founded upon a pre-understanding of action, and, in the ordinary way of talking, the propensity to relate the stories which happen to people, or those which they are caught up in, or simply the story of someone's life. Here, Ricoeur acknowledges the question of the notion of a pre-narrative structure of experience, and the 'objection about a vicious circle that haunts my whole analysis'[17] which will be taken up later.

Ricoeur's analysis of *Time and Narrative* is a major three-volume work in which he extensively analyses particularly the key themes of Augustine, Aristotle, Kant, Husserl and Heidegger.[18] However, it is not my aim to attempt to deal with all the critical features of this work, but simply to take account of those which relate to key issues. In the view that there is a recognition in action of temporal structures which call for narration, Ricoeur finds particular help from Heidegger's existential analysis in *Being and Time*. What Ricoeur is concerned to demonstrate is that the unity of historical time, the unity of abstract, linear clock time which is fundamental to description and discursive writing, is derived from the deep ontological unity of temporal being. For this reason, he claims that, although the ontological aim of *Being and Time* is the analysis of *Dasein* as the 'place'[19] where being is constituted through its capacity of posing the question or meaning of Being, it must first have a consistency with a philosophical anthropology if it is to achieve the ontological breakthrough that is expected of it.[19]

To this end, it is Heidegger's notion of 'within-time-ness' that he finds particularly helpful:

> I find the same powerful breakthrough in the analyses that conclude the study of temporality in the second division of *Being and Time*. These analyses are centred on our relation to time as that 'within which' we ordinarily act. This structure of within-time-ness (*Innerzeitigheit*) seems the best characterization of the temporality of action for my present analysis.
> (*Ibid.*, vol , p. 61)

What interests him most is the way Heidegger's analysis of within-time-ness makes *Dasein* a unity whereby a temporal unity is given to action in which 'future', 'past' and 'present' disappear, and time is figured as the exploded unity of the three temporal extases: coming to be, having been and making present.[21] This unity, which is based upon the dialectic between the extases, is what Heidegger defines as the constitution of Care (*Sorge*).[22] Care is an existential concept which is not an abstract measure. For example, a day is a period which corresponds to Care and the world in which it is the 'time do' something, where 'now' signifies 'now that ... '.

Within-time-ness is defined by this basic characteristic of Care. But although the description of temporality with respect to Care seems to make this dependent upon the description of things that are cared about, Heidegger's ontological definition of the constitution of Care attempts to prevent it from being determined by this ontic level of objects of Care. Care is constituted by the dialectic of coming to be, having been and making present, with the primacy given to the future over the present. As an existential concept it is directly related to the authenticity of self which may be defined in terms of the unity of self-identity, or the affirmation of the presence of the self. Ontologically, Care is directed toward the temporal horizon of the future; for Heidegger this is being-towards-death, although Ricoeur is critical of this view and claims that it is also being- towards-hope.[23] This temporal horizon must be looked at in the analysis of the act of the imagination in the way being appears, or is uncovered in the form of figuration. Here the concern is with a tension set up by Care as the dynamic of 'grasping' the horizon by means of a configured unity of narrative.

Existentially, the tension is between authenticity and inauthenticity, between the infinite possibilities of the temporal horizon of being and the threat of finitude and its ultimate 'weapon' of death; in other words, a tension between the affirmation and suspicion of presence. This tension is the condition of Sonorous Being phenomenologically manifested in the sonority of the lived body. Psychologically, it is experienced in the emotions, for example, in fear, anxiety, distress as well as hope, peace and contentment, being semantically mediated through sound patterns. At this level, Care is the emotional propensity to give meaning to these experiences in narrative form. The sound patterns of the narrative, the modulations, cadences, stress and pregnant moments of silence resonate with the emotional activity of the lived body and the sonority of being in the tension between chaotic discordance and the unified density of harmonic concordance. Care is the basic characteristic of within-time-ness which generates a dialectical tension to affirm self-identity in the telling and reading of stories.

Derridean Critique of Ontological Unity

However, before continuing with an analysis of Ricoeur's ontological viewpoint in his theory of narrative, it is important to note Derrida's critique of Heidegger's attempt to overcome the metaphysical presuppositions of traditional Western philosophy, and particularly the Kantian and Husserlian transcendental subject. In his essay 'The Ends of Man' in Margins of Philosophy, he points out that the 'formal structure' in which the question of Being is asked in Being and Time reveals that in the 'we' at the beginning of the text[24] Dasein is founded upon what Derrida calls phenomenology's principle of principles. That is, the method for the elaboration of the question of Being is

governed by ... the principle of presence, and of presence in self-presence, such as it is manifested to the being and in the being *we* are. It is this self-presence, this absolute proximity of the (questioning) being to itself, this familiarity with itself of the being ready to understand Being, that intervenes in the determination of the *factum*, and which motivates the choice of exemplary being, of the text, the good text for the hermeneutics of the meaning of Being ... The proximity to itself of the inquirer authorizes the identity of the inquirer and the interrogated.
(*Margins of Philosophy*, pp. 125–6)

If the implicit acceptance or affirmation of self-presence is assumed as the basis for the question of Being, it would seem that Heideggerian ontology has not resolved the problem of the source of unity whereby presence is affirmed. In pursuing Ricoeur's theory of narrative and narrative identity it may be found that there is no resolution to this problem in terms of the Derridean critique, but that one way to resolve the threat of 'closure'[25] is the hermeneutical approach based upon the dialectic between 'suspicion' and 'affirmation'.

Notes

1. See Aristotle's *Metaphysics*, Book IV, 1005b, 20. This is qualified with respect to temporality in *De Interpretatione*, Chapter 6, 17a, 30. Kant, although affirming the principle with respect to analytical judgements, reconsiders the Aristotelian temporal qualifier by supplementing the principle with a series of additional ones. See the entry on 'contradiction' in *A Kant Dictionary*, Howard Caygill, pp. 134–5. A radically different view is taken by Hegel in his *Logic* in relation to the dialectical movement of the becoming of Being. According to Hegel, everything is inherently contradictory. See the *Science of Logic*, tr. A.V. Miller, C. Contradiction *p*p. 431–43. It is this view which has influenced the developments in dialectical philosophy including Ricoeur and Derrida.
2. The separation of rational and poetic modes of language in the rational tradition of Western philosophy has its roots in the Platonic concern with 'truth'. For example, see Book X of the *Republic*. (See also, 'Plato on Poetic Creativity', Elizabeth Asmis, in *The Cambridge Companion to Plato*, ed. Richard Kraut.) Platonic idealism has not remained the only philosophical influence in the Western tradition. The commitment to the ideal of rational 'truth' free from poetic emotional contamination has continued dominant, particularly with respect to science. However, the radical questioning of the notion of 'truth' in all disciplines of modern philosophy has led to an increased interest in the role of poetry, especially in hermeneutic philosophy. For example, see *Contingency, Irony, and Solidarity* Richard Rorty. For a different perspective which aims at a greater integration between the rational and the poetic, see *Love's Knowledge*, Martha Nussbaum. Also, *A Ricoeur Reader:Reflection & Imagination*, ed. Mario I. Valdés.
3. See Study 8 of *The Rule of Metaphor* and the conclusions of *Time and Narrative*, vol. 3.
4. See 'The Linguistic Sign' in *Course in General Linguistics*, Part One, Chapter II, p. 65ff.

5. See chapter 2, *Of Grammatology*, tr. Gayatri C. Spivak.
6. The metaphorical reference is founded upon the symbolic characteristic of 'this *is* that'. Ricoeur retains the ontological *naïveté* of the metaphorical '*is*' in relation to a tensional view of metaphorical truth and literal truth by insisting upon the inclusion of the literal 'is not' within the ontological vehemence of the metaphorical 'is'. See *Rule of Metaphor*, pp. 247–56.
7. This is a reference to the descriptive statements clustered around an entity in terms of, for example, the representation of the objectified 'what' of Cartesian *realitas objectiva*, or the Kantian epistemologically inaccessible, intuited *Ding an sich*. See Heidegger's *The Basic Problems of Phenomenology*, pp. 34–8.
8. *Oneself as Another*, p. 315.
9. Merleau-Ponty's *The Visible and the Invisible* is unfinished and is a seminal work. Consequently, the references to 'sonorous being' are not part of a defined ontology. Furthermore, his work on the linguistic implications is incomplete, and does not address the issue of the written text. Nevertheless, he provides valuable insights into nature of the lived body and sonority as a key characteristic.
10. Dylan Thomas writes about poetry and words, and the first poems read to him as a child: 'What mattered most was the *sound* of them … And these words were, to me, as the notes of bells, the sounds of musical instruments, the noises of wind, the rattle of milk carts, the clopping of hooves on cobbles, the fingering of branches on a window pane, might be to someone, deaf from birth, who has miraculously found his hearing.' 'Notes on the Art of Poetry' in *Modern Poets on Modern Poetry*, ed. James Sculley.
11. This notion of 'grasping' has its roots in the Kantian act of synthesis. Kant consistently relates this either to 'power of the imagination, a blind but indispensable function of the soul, without which we should have no knowledge whatsoever, but of which we are scarcely ever conscious' (*CPR* A78/B103), or to 'an act of spontaneity of the faculty of representation' or 'an act of the self-activity of the subject' (B130).
12. In his concern with the human condition and the disciplines of the human sciences, Ricoeur clearly acknowledges his work in terms of a philosophical anthropology particularly in his early work, *Fallible Man*. But also in his later work, for example, *Time and Narrative*, when he is sensitive to the accusation of interpreting Heidegger's *Being and Time* from the viewpoint of philosophical anthropology and failing to apprehend the anti-metaphysical critique of this work (vol. 3 pp. 60–61), he claims that an attentive reading may discern features of the present which do not reflect the alleged errors of intuitive metaphysics. If this is combined with his criticism of Heidegger's failure, according to Ricoeur, to return to the level of rational discourse, it reveals his insistent philosophical anthropological aim to establish a foundation for the human sciences.
13. See conclusion to Kant's *Critique of Practical Reason*, tr. Lewis White Beck, pp. 169–71.
14. See *Time and Narrative*, Vol. 1, pp. 54–71.
15. See *Time and Narrative*, Vol. 1, chapter 2. Also, Ricoeur's essay, 'Life in Quest of a Narrative' in *On Paul Ricoeur: Narrative and Interpretation*, ed. David Wood.
16. See Ricoeur's comments on the 'symbolic resources of the practical field' in *Time and Narrative*, Vol. 1, pp. 57–8.

17. *Time and Narrative*, Vol. 1, p. 60. See Ricoeur's response, pp. 71–6.
18. In particular, as they relate to the relationship between historical, or 'lived' time, and linear, or 'cosmic' time.
19. See Addendum to 'The Origin of the Work of Art', *Basic Writings*, pp. 207–12.
20. See note 25.
21. See Being and Time, pp. 326–8.
22. Ibid., p. 284ff.
23. See time and Narrative, Vol. 3, pp. 135–6.
24. See p. 123ff.
25. See note 26, Chapter 1.

Chapter 4

Prose Rhythm: the Mediation of Sonorous Being

Sonority and Ontological Unity

The significance of sonority with respect to metaphor and narrative is the role it plays as a textual mode of mediation of the ontological grounding of identity. Sound is the centripetal dynamic of the iconic moment, that is, the symbolic unity of metaphor, and the mimetic configuration of narrative whereby univocity is achieved. But if sonority, in terms of the phonetic characteristics of metaphor and narrative, is expressive of an ontologically grounded identity, a unity of self, what does it manifest about the nature of that ontological grounding? If unity is achieved, that is, if identity is affirmed through the textual mediation based upon dynamic sonority, what is the ontological nature of this dynamic? If the affirmation of identity is mediated through the mode of the text which is ontologically grounded, the source of this identity must be ontological. But this, for example, according to Derrida, is where the problem lies.

Ontological Unity and Heidegger's Question of Being

Derrida is critical of Heidegger's approach to this issue of ontological unity. He points to the 'we' in the text of *Sein und Zeit* as revealing the unquestioned transcendental subject even in this radical attempt to disclose the grounding of Being.[1] The 'we' provokes the question, is this an identity based upon an assumed unity of Being in Heidegger's ontology? In spite of his careful concern to make clear that *Dasein* is not to be confused with the self-conscious subject,[2] Heidegger does not appear to address the question, *who* conducts the analysis? Heidegger's aim is to uncover the Being upon which the 'who' is grounded; that the analysis, as it were, may turn back upon itself to reveal the ground upon which it is conducted. But, in so doing, he adopts an unquestioned perspective which, even though it is critically examined in the process of the analysis, may invalidate the disclosure.[3] Is it not necessary to address the prior question: who, or what, is the 'who' who asks the question which instigates the analysis? This is prior to the question, 'what is the meaning of Being?' which Heidegger poses at the beginning of *Sein und Zeit*, because to pose the question is to assume the 'who'. How then is it possible to pose any question? This would seem to be the fundamental dilemma of any philosophic enterprise.[4]

Heidegger poses the question of Being in initiating his attempt to uncover the ground of the *who*, but is it not the 'who' who poses the question which is revealed by the 'we' in the text? In an attempt to uncover not only the identity of the 'who' who makes this attempt, but the ontological grounding of this identity, how is it possible to begin such an attempt without assuming an unquestioned grounding? Heidegger's attempt is to strip away all phenomenological and ontological assumptions, and begin with the question, 'What is the meaning of Being?', and let the question be; that is, let the question, in terms of its internal dynamic, determine and direct the process of disclosure of Being. In this process, the 'who' who attempts to lay bare the question of Being is disturbed and deconstructed. That is, the 'who' who seemingly appears in self-consciousness through the mediation of reflection is radically questioned in the ontological disclosure.[5]

The Primordial Dialectic of Temporal Being

The dynamic and form of this questioning arising from the fundamental question of Being is existential, and not based upon traditional Western logic.[6] This is evident in the way Heidegger understands that the fundamental question is basic to the experience of life in all circumstances. In *An Introduction to Metaphysics*, where he poses the question in the form, 'Why are there essents rather than nothing?', acknowledging that many never encounter this question, he writes,

> And yet each of us is grazed at least once, perhaps more than once, by the hidden power of this question, even if he is not aware of what is happening to him. The question looms in moments of great despair, when things tend to lose all their weight and all meaning becomes obscured. Perhaps it will strike but once like a muffled bell that rings into our life and gradually dies away. It is present in moments of rejoicing, when all things around us are transfigured and seem to be there for the first time, as if it might be easier to think they are not than to understand that they are and as they are. The question is upon us in boredom, when we are equally removed from despair and joy, and everything about us seems hopelessly commonplace that we no longer care whether anything is or is not – and with the question 'Why are there essents rather than nothing?' is evoked in a particular form.
> (*An Introduction to Metaphysics*, p. 1–2)

The question 'is evoked in a particular form'. It is a form expressive of an existential condition arising from the 'hidden power of the question' rooted in a state of Being. From this Heideggerian ontological perspective, the condition of being-in-the-world is disclosed in the existential questioning which manifests a hidden power. It is this perspective which provides the way to develop an analysis of textual sonority, and attempt a resolution of the problematic of ontological unity. It is in relation to the sonorous dynamic of the narrative mode of the text that Derrida's critique needs to be addressed, to show that this dynamic sonority, grounded in the hidden power of being-in-the-world, is the key characteristic of narrative identity as the mediation of the 'who' who questions.

The question of Being arising from its hidden power is essentially dialectical between suspicion and affirmation of identity, or presence. On the one hand, identity is always under suspicion. In the condition of constant temporal flux of being-in-the-world, there is the propensity of endless questioning so that suspicion is never lifted. On the other hand, identity is affirmed in the activity of being-in-the-world through the mediation of textual narrative. There is a moment of suspension of, or release from, the questioning, but not an escape from suspicion. Existentially, on the one side of the dialectic, suspicion may be expressed in terms of distress, insecurity, anxiety, and the threat of insanity; and, on the other, affirmation in terms of hope, belonging, peace and meaningfulness.

Sound and the Primordial Dialectic[7]

What is the ontological condition from which the power of this dialectic originates, and how is sonority a manifestation of this state? The issue here, from the Heideggerian perspective outlined above, is the mediation of the 'who' through the appearance and expression of the primordial dialectic in the narrative text. Sound, in terms of sentence and discourse, is the expression of temporal Being; that is, the expression of the activity of being-in-the-world. Furthermore, it is sound that is the inherent characteristic of the phenomenological intentional process of figuration and configuration. If temporal Being is dialectical, does this sonorous characteristic of narrative disclose the ontological nature of the primordial dialectic? If the ontological primordial dialectic is existentially expressed in distress and hope, insecurity and belonging, anxiety and peace, chaos and unity, insanity and meaning, suspicion and affirmation, what does textual sonority disclose about the primordial dialectic as the grounding of this existential expression?[7]

The Dialectic of Self and Other

Textual sonority, in terms of phonic modulations, cadences and resonance, is the dynamic of convergence in terms of configuration. The sounds not simply of the words but expressions of sentences and the whole narrative discourse in reading and appropriating the *Lebenswelt* of the text is the intentional dynamic of the plot and its various narrative features. It is the dynamic of phenomenological intentionality,[8] a dynamic of sonority resulting from the dialectic of the self who reads and appropriates the world of the narrative, and the identity of that world which may be called the other-than-self, the 'who' of the text. It is the dialectic of the self reflecting upon the discursive, descriptive mode of the narrative seeking rational explanations, and the self imaginatively responding to the world of the narrative, in seeking to appropriate its identity in understanding. This dialectic, manifested in textual sonority, is the dialectic of an activity between reflection and understanding, a reverberation of the relationship between self and other grounded in temporal Being.[9]

The mark of self-consciousness is the irresistible propensity to affirm its identity through reflection which is stained with indelible suspicion. There is no end to questioning. And yet, affirmation is paradoxically only possible where the interrogation is relinquished in letting go self-consciousness; that is, when self is absorbed in the narrative identity, the other, in the 'who' of the text. But affirmation is essentially an act of self-consciousness. It is intrinsically the achievement of reflection? If it were not, how would it be possible to define affirmation? What would affirmation mean? Herein lies the paradox which must be given close and careful examination. The crucial and central issue is textual sonority as the active manifestation of the dynamic set up in the appropriation of the narrative in the dialectic between the self and the other-than-self, or the 'who' of the text. It is the moments of intensity in which the dialectic of reflection and the absorption of self in the other is manifested in sonority rooted in the reverberations of the phenomenological lived body and ontologically grounded in temporal Being.

In the act of reading, there is the process of reflection in which the reader takes up the mode of self-consciousness[10] which is the distancing of self and object, of subjectivity and objectivity, as the space of abstraction whereby logical interrogation is made possible. The reader, as it were, stands back from the text consciously aware of the relationship of self with the text. Existentially, the ground of this interrogation is the dialectic of distress and hope, anxiety and peace, insecurity and belonging, chaos and unity, insanity and meaning, suspicion and affirmation. The hidden power of reflective questioning is manifested in the dialectic between the reflective process of rational explanation which can never be closed, and the imaginative act of understanding.[11] The appearance of temporal Being is marked by the propensity of distress, anxiety, insecurity, chaos, insanity and suspicion through its hidden power manifested in the interrogation of the reflection of self. Reflection is grounded in the ontologically interrogative hidden power that is released by the appearance of temporal Being.[12] But authentic interrogation cannot be closed, therefore appearance is always subject to suspicion. The inevitable consequence of authentic interrogation is the questioning of the self who questions; and even the explicit or implicit interrogation of Dasein. Suspicion can only be lifted if the 'who' who questions is beyond questioning, or if questioning is relinquished at the moment of affirmation – the moment when the self is lost in the 'who' of the text.

Textually, it is the patterned, or rhythmic sonority precipitated in the appropriation of the narrative that effects an intentional convergence in an intensity of resonance[13] rooted in Sonorous Being. This rhythmic sonority is essentially the key characteristic of the poetic mode in contrast to the predominantly rational, discursive mode. In particular, it is the metaphoric and narrative features of this mode which effect the levels of intensity. Such an intensity of resonance, set up by an appropriation of the text, is an oscillation within the dynamic of the primordial dialectic between self and other, between suspicion and affirmation. It is the moment when self is lost in the 'who' of the text, but 'in the blink of an eye' (*Augenblick*) there is distance and interrogation. Following the moment, the stain of suspicion retains an indelible resonance of hope.

The appearance of temporal Being is mediated in the act of configuration made possible by the rhythmic sonority of the text. It is held in the moment of the act in a teleological, dialectical intensity of suspicion and affirmation. Sound is the essential characteristic of its presence. However, sound is integrally related to all sensible activity of the lived body which is affected by the reverberations of temporal Being in the creative process of its appearance in the historical activity of human beings. It is the textual mediation of the poetic mode which may uniquely affirm the appearance.

Textual Sonority and Ontological Unity

Sound, as an intrinsic characteristic of language, plays a key role in the linguistic mediation of ontologically grounded identity. Although it is the givenness of the text in terms of the linguistic sign system that is basic to the structuring of consciousness, sound is fundamental in the process of appropriation of the text and the affirmation of identity. To read a text is to pronounce, to utter, to articulate audibly or silently.[14] Although the linguistic sign system of the text is primary, sound, in the act of reading, is key to the affirmation of narrative identity and, consequently, conceptual unity.

The poetic mode of the text, which includes poetry and narrative discourse, reveals that sound is fundamental in the appropriation of the text based upon the hermeneutical understanding that appropriation is defined in terms of inhabiting the world, the *Lebenswelt* of the text. More particularly, it is the textual rhythmic structures of sound that are the characteristic features of this appropriation.

Prose Rhythm

In their work on *Mimesis*,[15] Gunter Gebauer and Christoph Wulf examine the way the role of the voice was dominant in ancient Greek society and culture, and the continuing influence of this view since that time, in particular referring to the anthropological investigation of Jesper Svenbro in his *Phraseikleia*.[16] They write,

> In terms of the early Greek attitude toward writing, which regards what is written but not spoken, the unread text, as incomplete, the structural linking of writing with the act of reading is constitutive for the text: the reading is part of the text.'...
> From this point of view, the text requires the reader's temporal investment; reading is not a private process, but belongs to the reader and to the text. 'If he lends his voice to these mute signs, the text appropriates it: his voice becomes the voice of the written text.'...
> (*Mimesis*, p. 201)

In the act of audible or silent reading the sound of the voice plays a key role in the appropriation, the habitation of the *Lebenswelt* of the text through the 'grasping' of the mimetic configuration of the plot.

Northrop Frye identifies an important characteristic of the relationship of sound to the text in what he calls, 'prose rhythm'.[18] In his *Anatomy of Criticism*, he proposes that there is a fundamental relationship between event and idea, between verbal imitations of actions and thought with respect to literature – in Aristotelian terms, between *ethos* and *dianoia*.[18] According to Frye, this is the first aspect of the diagrammatic framework that has been used in poetics since the time of Aristotle. He writes,

> The world of social action and event, the world of time and process, has a particularly close association with the ear. The ear listens, and the ear translates what it hears into practical conduct.
> (*Anatomy of Criticism*, p. 243)

Drawing upon the list of elements of poetry in Aristotle's *Poetics*,[19] he proceeds to examine the second or rhetorical aspect of literature:

> Considered as a verbal structure, literature presents a lexis which combines two other elements: *melos*, an element analogous to or otherwise connected with music, and *opsis*, which has a similar connection with the plastic arts. The word *lexis* itself may be translated 'diction' when we are thinking of it as a narrative sequence of sounds caught by the ear, and as 'imagery' when we are thinking of it as forming a simultaneous pattern of meaning apprehended in an act of mental 'vision'.
> (*Ibid.*, p. 244)

Frye's notion of prose rhythm is a development of poetic rhythm. He writes,

> In every poem we can hear at least two distinct rhythms. One is the recurring rhythm, which we have shown to be a complex of accent, metre, and sound-pattern.

The other is the semantic rhythm of sense, or what is usually felt to be the prose rhythm ... We have verse *epos* when the recurrent rhythm is primary or organizing one, and prose when the semantic rhythm is primary.
(*Ibid.*, p. 263)

Prose rhythm, in contrast to the recurring rhythm of poetry, is a transparent medium. It is at its best 'when it is the least obtrusive and presents its subject-matter like plate glass in a shop window'. As examples of this, Frye cites the long sentences of the later novels of Henry James, and the working backwards and forwards of Joseph Conrad's writing as the way the *melos*, the prose rhythm is designed to shift the attention from listening to looking at the central situation through a visual metaphor. The process is reversible in, for example, according to Frye, the dislocations of the narrative in *Tristram Shandy* which have the effect of taking the attention away from looking at the external situation to listening to the process of its coming into being in the author's mind.

It is the crucial role of sound in this act of habitation, in terms of Frye's notion of prose rhythm, that provides the grounding of this act as the essential mediation of activity in this process of habitation. According to Frye, sound is the *melos*, the element of diction which translates practical conduct.[20] The world of the narrative is a state of activity, and to inhabit that world is actively to appropriate its ontological unified perspective. This includes particular activity in terms of characters and the unfolding plot: incidents, events and behaviour. Through habitation, the reader is there in the world alongside or inside the characters, actively engaging with their world. Although subsidiary to the plot (*mythos*), perhaps more fundamentally it is the *ethos* in terms of atmosphere, mood, tone and tenor of the world which is the active grounding of the habitation.[21] For it is this *ethos* which is the active disturbance of the reader's consciousness existentially expressed in terms of emotional states of being. An example would be the *ethos* of the first chapter of Thomas Hardy's *Return of the Native* in the powerful description of Egdon Heath which remains as the perspective of the whole novel; or the description of Lincoln Cathedral in Chapter 7 of D.H. Lawrence's The Rainbow. Prose rhythm is the background, in terms of *ethos*, to the poetic rhythm of the figurative visual images, and is a critical integral influence upon the latter. Furthermore, as Frye claims, prose rhythm is most effective when it is the least obtrusive.

Among the characteristics of prose rhythm[22] there are, for example, in Hardy's description of Egdon Heath, the intensity of a rhythm mediated by the long vowel sounds, and the stress that has the propensity of a downwards tonal direction. For example,

The face of the heath by its mere complexion added half an hour to the evening; it could in like manner retard the dawn, sadden the moon, anticipate the frowning of storms scarcely generated, and intensify the opacity of a moonless midnight to a cause of shaking and dread.
(*Return of the Native*, p. 33)

In contrast, Lawrence's description stresses a tonal uplift, combining the effect of the rounded vowel with the short vowel to mediate a sense of inhabiting Will Brangwen's active state of being as he enters the cathedral:

> Here the stone leapt up from the plain of earth, leapt up in a manifold, clustered desire each time, up, away from the horizontal earth, through twilight and dusk the whole range of desire, through the swerving, the declination, ah, to the ecstasy, the touch, to the meeting and the consummation, the meeting, the clasp, the close embrace, the neutrality, the perfect, swooning, consummation, the timeless ecstasy. There his soul remained, at the apex of the arch, clinched in the timeless ecstasy, consummated.
>
> (*The Rainbow*, p. 202)

Other characteristics of prose rhythm include the descriptive interactions in terms of a resonance that mediates an actual effect in, for example, Joseph Conrad's *The Heart of Darkness*. In his critical study of this novel in *The Great Tradition*, F.R. Leavis attempts to demonstrate the way the same vocabulary that Conrad uses to convey the mysteriousness of the Congo also applied to the evocation of human profundities and spiritual horrors; in particular, in the passage when Marlow is startled by being suddenly confronted with shrunken heads on stakes, symbolic of the invasion of the wilderness in the darkness of Kurtz's heart. Leavis writes,

> The essential vibration emanates from the interaction of the particular incidents, actions, and perceptions that are evoked with such charged concreteness. The legitimate kind of comment, that which seems the inevitable immediate resonance of the recorded event, is represented here:
>
> (*The Great Tradition*, p. 205)

The passage he then quotes begins,

> And then I made a brusque movement, and one of the remaining posts of that vanished fence leaped into the field of my glass ...

The elements of prose rhythm, however, include a range of linguistic characteristics each having the particular effects dependent upon the way in which they are employed in the text. Even when a novel is translated from one language to another, depending upon the ability of the translator to be able to listen critically in both languages, the prose rhythm may, for example, through the structure of sentences and discourse, create the same relevant effects in terms of inhabiting the *Lebenswelt* of the narrative.[23] The continual diversions and meandering discourse of Marcel Proust's *A la recherche du temps perdu*, with its convoluted sentences and multiple subordinate clauses, has the effect of a rhythm insistently prompting the reader to inhabit the world of the hero and the narrator in which the exploration and search in time and memory along Swann's Way and The Guermantes Way evokes their resolution in 'Time Regained'. It is a prose rhythm that grounds what Gilles Deleuze calls an 'apprenticeship to signs'[24] in an ontological resonance which, for example, roots the visual image of the 'madeleine cake' in the particular activity of hero's childhood, and the way the constant presence of that activity resonates and decisively influences his search in time and memory.

Prose rhythm is what the reader hears in a way similar to the background noises of human activity in the habitation of a social world. It is this background which is the ontological setting for particular conscious activity. It is in relation to this background that the experiences of distress and hope, insecurity and belonging, anxiety and peace are expressed. In reading, there is a listening that has a focus of attention effected by the acoustical background, which may be compared to Merleau-Ponty's understanding of the configuration of perception.[25] This is set up in the act of appropriation in the way that sound patterns of the prose rhythm are animated through the visual element of appropriation: the sight of the textual signs initiates the process of listening creating the acoustical background of the reader's consciousness. The reader's visual and acoustical response to the text animates the prose rhythm which is the manifestation of his sonorous condition of being in the process of inhabiting the *Lebenswelt* of the narrative; an active condition of being that is phenomenologically expressed in the acoustical resonance affecting the whole of the 'lived' body.

Prose Rhythm as Phonic Texture

Merleau-Ponty's phenomenological analysis of perception provides a valuable way of understanding this habitation. For Merleau-Ponty the body is not simply an objective organism among others in the world. It is the phenomenological medium of consciousness whereby the self is incarnated in a *Lebenswelt*.[26] The appearance of the *Lebenswelt* is a process of habitation whereby the body is the medium of external perception. He writes,

> The thing, and the world, are given to me along with the parts of my body, not by any 'natural geometry, but in living connection, or rather identical, with that existing between the parts of my body itself.
> (*Phenomenology of Perception*, p. 205)

For example, when the right hand grasps the left hand, the latter is perceived objectively through the medium of touch of the former which may in 'the blink of an eye' be reversed. In Merleau- Ponty's view, this is a basic dialectic of the interdependence of subjectivity and objectivity within the consciousness of the habitation of the 'lived' body.[27]

To inhabit the world of a narrative is to inhabit language understood as an expressive texture of *phonetic gesture* whereby the phenomenal body is aroused by the voice.[28] He writes,

Speech always comes into play against a background of speech; it is always only a fold in the immense fabric of language. To understand it, we do not have to consult some inner lexicon which gives us pure thoughts covered up by words or forms we are perceiving; we only have to lend ourselves to its life, to its movement of differentiation and articulation, and to its eloquent gestures.

(*Signs*, p. 42)

This does not take account of prose rhythm, and approaches the fabric of language in terms of living speech rather than the written text. It is, however, Merleau-Ponty's understanding of phonetic gesture that provides the way of understanding the phenomenological and ontological role of phonicity in the appropriation of the text by the reader. He writes,

The phonetic 'gesture' brings about, both for the speaking subject and for his hearers, a certain structural co-ordination of experience, exactly as a pattern of my bodily behaviour endows the objects around me with a certain significance both for me and for others. The meaning of the gesture is not contained in it like some physical or physiological phenomenon. The meaning of the word is not contained in the sound. But the human body is defined in terms of its property of appropriating, in an indefinite series of acts, significant cores which transcend and transfigure its natural powers. The act of transcendence is first encountered in the acquisition of a pattern of behaviour, then in the mute communication of gesture: it is the same power that the body opens itself to some new kind of conduct and makes it understood to external witnesses.

(*Phenomenology of Perception*, p. 193)

The fabric of language as a phonetic system as the structure of habitation through which the phonetic gesture is made.

Reading involves listening to the phonetic texture that is animated by the imaginative activity of the *Lebenswelt* of the narrative mediated through the written sign system. Appropriation of the narrative in terms of habitation involves a resonance of prose rhythm arising from a change in state of being; a resonance which permeates the active 'lived' body. It is this resonance which is imaginatively translated into the background activity of the inhabited *Lebenswelt*; and which makes possible the phonetic gesture of those particular activities which are the focus of attention. To inhabit a text is to appropriate a phonetic texture, a prose rhythm which is the manifestation of a sonorous state of being. It is a state of being arising from a hidden ontological power effected by the primordial dialectic of self and other in the process of reading.

Sonority and Narrative Identity: Corporeal Intentionality

Reading a narrative is to corporeally inhabit its *Lebenswelt* in which there is a bodily resonance set up by appropriation of the prose rhythm of the text. It is this resonance that is the medium of the reader's condition of being in the process of habitation effecting an ontological hidden power expressed through corporeal resonance in terms of dynamic convergence.[29] Following Merleau-Ponty's understanding of the 'lived' body in phenomenological terms, that is, corporeal levels of consciousness,[30] this dynamic convergence is called *corporeal intentionality*. Relating this notion to the act of reading, the 'lived' body is engaged in the reader's grasp of the narrative. Corporeal intentionality is fundamental to understanding the meaning of the text, and the appropriation of a narrative identity.

'Operative' and 'Particular' Intentionality

Prose rhythm is, however, only one feature of corporeal intentionality. It is the background to the reader's habitation of the text. It is the sound which the reader may be relatively unaware of as he follows the narrative plot. His attention is given to the particular action which is the focus of intentional convergence. But, according to Merleau-Ponty, this focus, the grasping of the meaning of the particular action is made possible by the background which he calls *operative* intentionality in contrast to *particular* intentionality.[31] It is the dialectical relationship of these two which is corporeal intentionality. In *Phenomenology of Perception*, he defines perception as 'the background against which all acts and interpretations stand out'. Perception is the way the world is inhabited in terms of consciousness. It is the totality of conscious experience including all that is received through the senses. Developing this view, he draws upon Gestalt theory of psychology. He writes,

> The Gestalt psychologists have shown ... the world presents itself at each instance as a meaningful totality in which moments possess their sense as they function in the whole spectacle to which they contribute.
> (*Merleau-Ponty's Critique of Reason*, Thomas Langan, p. 29)

For example, attention given to a book lying on a table is to be conscious of its being a book in terms of its shape, colour, size, title, etc. But for this conscious attention, when a particular object appears as an object in consciousness, there must be a background – the room which is not directly experienced, at the moment of attention on the particular object, as, for example, individual colours, shapes, lines, etc., but is nevertheless part of consciousness. The attentive act, particular intentionality, is made possible by operative intentionality which structures the whole: the whole of conscious awareness which, other than the particular focus of attention, makes this attentive focus possible; it is operative in the sense that the particular object and activity dynamically emerge from this background. The book is not an isolated object; it lies on the table which may be viewed from many different perspectives in the room where the table is. Each perspective is contextual and determines the appearance of the book. Each perspective is operative with respect to an intentionality that makes the particular intentionality possible.

Particular Intentionality and Metaphoric Phonicity

The most effective parts of the texts, with regard to the reader's grasp of narrative identity through particular intentionality, is the phonicity of the metaphoric features of the narrative. Sound here grounds the reader's attention in particular concrete actions since the phonicity of the iconic moment of metaphor is dominant, in contrast to the conceptual syntax of the descriptive passages.[32] It is therefore a more direct mediation of particular actions. Like the beat of a drum which is immediately translated into bodily movement, the phonicity of the iconic moment of metaphor is translated into corporeal resonance effecting habitation of the particular actions whereby the reader is conscious of these actions in a concrete mode.

An example of reading Will and Anna Brangwen's experience of Lincoln Cathedral in D.H. Lawrence's *The Rainbow* reveals the way prose rhythm effects the habitation of the narrative. This selected chapter should not of course be separated from the whole novel, and a more detailed criticism would take account of this. The focus upon the relationship of Will and Anna in their experience of the Cathedral must be understood with regard to the theme of the psychological exploration of marriage across three generations in which the Lebenswelt of the novel has many facets.[33] Nevertheless, the appropriation of each facet may be examined in terms of habitation and the particular and operative aspects of corporeal intentionality. Particular intentionality relates to the reader's focus of attention with respect to the cathedral as experienced by Will and Anna. This focus is not static but moves through the chapter with the reader at times alongside them, and at critical moments within one or the other. Habitation means that the reader appropriates a focus of attention through the description of the experience of the particular characters. For example, the reader appropriates the sight of the cathedral in the distance through Will's experience:

> When he saw the cathedral in the distance, dark blue lifted watchful in the sky, his heart leapt. It was the sign in heaven, it was the Spirit hovering like a dove, like an eagle over the earth. He turned his glowing, ecstatic face to her, his mouth opened with a strange, ecstatic grin.
> (*The Rainbow*, p. 200)

Because the particular focus is part of the unfolding narrative, it may include different levels of the reader's critical awareness. Will and Anna's experience of the cathedral is a critical moment in the psychological exploration of the relationship, and their failure, from the perspective of the novel, to achieve individual fulfilment. For Will, who seeks fulfilment in his security and comfort in Anna and his work, and is afraid of the unknown, the cathedral is the symbol of everything which he holds valuable in life,[34] but for Anna

> it was the ultimate confine ... The altar was barren, its lights gone out. God burned no more in that bush. It was dead matter lying there. She claimed the right to freedom above her, higher than the roof.
> (*Ibid.*, p. 203)

These narrative interpretations are part of the novel's exploration that the reader appropriates in the imaginative act of inhabiting its *Lebenswelt* which will be dialectically related to the reader's self-identity in everyday life. Inhabiting the experience of Will and Anna in which there are critical levels of awareness appropriated from the narrative creates a critical tension in the dialectic between the narrative and the reader's self-identity. In other words, the narrative may cause the reader to reflect upon principles, values and meanings which have been accepted as the basis for his or her self-identity.[35]

Although the focus of attention is held by the descriptions of Will and Anna's experience of the cathedral, it is given particular intensity in terms of an imaginative concreteness of their experience in the metaphoric characteristic of these descriptions. For example,

> Then he pushed open the door, and the great, pillared gloom was before him, in which his soul shuddered and rose from her nest. His soul leapt, soared up into the great church. His body stood still, absorbed by the height. His soul leapt up into the gloom, into possession, it reeled, it swooned with a great escape, it quivered in the womb, in the hush and gloom of fecundity, like seed of procreation in ecstacy.
> (*Ibid.*, p. 201)

The metaphors which express Will's experience, with respect to the condition of his soul as he enters the building, give an imaginative concreteness to the appropriation of that experience. That is, the reader's experience of the cathedral through an imaginative appropriation of the narrative description is not that of a passive observer but as one who inhabits the condition of Will's soul. 'Shuddered', 'leapt', 'soared', 'reeled', 'swooned', 'quivered' give to the imaginative focus of attention a concrete experience of the cathedral.

The habitation of the reader is intensified. His condition of being is affected by an ontological vehemence in the imaginative appropriation of the metaphorical images giving rise to a hidden power expressed in the dynamic of a phenomenological convergence, an intentionality with respect to the focus of attention.

Sound and image are dominant in metaphor because it is the intuitive perception of the similarity of dissimilars.[36] The imaginative grasp is immediate, not mediated through cognition but structuring conscious appearance through the mediation of linguistic acoustical modulations which are the objective materiality of the linguistic image. 'His soul leapt, soared up into the great church'. The reader's attention is given to the imaginative perception of the interior of the cathedral through the particular experience of Will Brangwen expressed in the metaphors, 'leapt' and 'soared'. The sound of these metaphors is the expression of the concrete experience which shapes the image of the building at the particular moment of the reader's attention. The sound is immediate and draws upon the phonic texture of the cultural linguistic structure of the reader's Lebenswelt grounded in the symbolic structuring of cultural human activity.[37] The phonicity of the metaphors 'leapt' and 'soared' have cultural associations with a sense of being lifted up, of overcoming, of expansiveness, of transcending the everyday affairs of life. Therefore, the sight of the interior of the cathedral through Will's particular experience is an image of awe, wonder and spiritual inspiration.

In contrast, the reader's attention is taken through the experience of Anna by means of metaphors which resonate with a different sound, and the cathedral is changed in the concrete perception of the reader:

> The altar was barren, its lights gone out. God burned no more in that bush. She claimed the right to freedom above her, higher than the roof. She had always a sense of being caved in.
> (*Ibid.*, p. 203)

In the continuing counterpointing of these contrasting experiences, the reader's focus of attention is led by the metaphorical structuring of the narrative to grasp the concrete image of the chapter's ultimate moment of activity, and to understand how their shared experience of the cathedral had affected their relationship:

> As he sat sometimes very still, with a bright, vacant face, Anna could see the suffering among the brightness. He was aware of some limit of himself, of something unformed in his very being, of some buds which were not ripe in him, some folded centres of darkness which would never develop and unfold whilst he was alive in the body. He was unready for fulfilment. Something undeveloped in him limited him, there was a darkness in him which he could not unfold, which would never unfold in him.
> (*Ibid.*, p. 210)

Although the passage is saturated with metaphor, 'bright, vacant face', 'suffering among the brightness' and 'folded centres of darkness' are the most vivid and resonate with a greater intensity. The dissonance between 'bright' and 'vacant', and 'suffering' and 'brightness' resonates with a sense of stifled vitality; and 'folded ... darkness' is an experience of the disturbance of repressed power. The passage reveals the way the focus of attention of particular intentionality, of Will sitting in a chair at the end of the day, is at the centre of a convergence of concentric circles of phonicity. Because the other metaphors are less vivid, less surprising, more conventional, the sounds have a tendency to 'fall away' into the background of the phonicity of the conceptual descriptive syntax as part of the prose rhythm. For example, 'some buds which were not ripe in him' is clearly a metaphor, but has a conventional familiarity which makes it sound more integrally part of the description,

> He was aware of some limit of himself, of something unformed in his very being, of some buds which were not ripe in him …
>
> (*Ibid.*, p. 210)

Prose Rhythm and Temporal Experience

To appropriate the particular actions of the passage, to inhabit the experience of Will and Anna and grasp the meaning of that experience, the reader must inhabit the time of the narrative. This is not simply clock time, the passage of minutes and hours, but the 'human' time of Will and Anna. What does 'human' time mean? Firstly, it is a time of activity. In the words of the preacher,

> a time to be born, and a time to die;
> a time to plant, and a time to pluck up what is planted;
> a time to kill, and a time to heal;
> a time to break down, and a time to build up;
> a time to weep, and a time to laugh;
> a time for war, and a time for peace.
>
> …
>
> (*Ecclesiastes*, 3.2–9)

'Human' time is defined in terms of activity.

Secondly, 'human' time is always time that is experienced. For example, it may be experienced as short, or fleeting in times of pleasure, joy and happiness; or it may be experienced as long and delayed in times of sadness or frustration, such as waiting to be discharged from hospital. 'Human' time is an emotional experience: there is a time of ecstasy, a time of distress, a time of peace, a time of anxiety, a time of satisfaction, a time of disappointment. There is never any 'human' time when the emotions are not affected in one way or another. Furthermore, emotional experience is expressed in bodily activity. The body resonates with emotional experience and is readily and spontaneously translated into sound and vice versa. This is why music is an expression of mood and emotion, and involuntarily precipitates bodily activity. 'Human' time is a corporeal resonance of emotional experience.

Appropriation of the 'human' time of the cathedral chapter is a habitation of its mood which is an experience of its temporality. As mentioned above, the ubiquitous long vowels with the predominance of tonal uplift, particularly with respect to Will's experience, express a patterned phonicity that is translated into corporeal activity which mediates his experience. In contrast to Will, and as a counterpoint, Anna's experience is mediated through vowel sounds that are shortened and the tone lowered; but the counterpointing makes the sounds of the total mood more subtle mediating a complex experience of their relationship which includes a deepening of mutual understanding combined with frustration and struggle. This interpretation, of course, to some extent, benefits from reflection upon the images and descriptive passages. Nevertheless, such reflection reveals the critical part played by the prose rhythm in appropriating the 'human' time of the chapter. It is this appropriation which gives the focus of attention of particular intentionality the dynamic convergence necessary for establishing a dialectical relationship between the reader and the unity of the narrative, between the reader's self-identity and the narrative ideniy, between self and other.

Inhabiting 'human' time is an appropriation of the unity of temporal experience. The chronology of the narrative may, of course, unfold in different ways. For example, in linear fashion of clock time whether on a daily basis or longer periods; or from multiple perspectives of a particular character; or perspectives upon the experiences of different characters. Nevertheless, the *Lebenswelt* of the narrative is one; and it is this unity that the reader appropriates, because it is this unity that determines the basis of the plot. The experience of temporal unity in the process of habitation by the reader is mediated through the operative intentionality of prose rhythm, but this is not the source of this unity. Merleau-Ponty claims that the unity of the objective world is constituted by the mind based upon the consciousness of the phenomenal activity of the 'lived' body which mediates a 'pre-constituted'.world.[38] The body, he writes, '… must teach me to comprehend what no constituting consciousness can know – my involvement in a 'pre-constituted' world'. It is the active habitation of the 'lived' body in the world which gives a phenomenological unity to the body prompting the mind to re-constitute this unity in reflection. Obviously, this is a movement into the Heideggerian ontological notion of being-in-the-world, but does not resolve the problem of ontological unity stated earlier. The hidden ontological power that is released in the appearance of being with respect to the primordial dialectic between self and other is the source of this unity. In terms of reading the textual narrative, it is the dialectic between the self-identity of the reader and the other, or 'who' of the narrative. Prose rhythm is the mediation of this primordial dialectic. The reader's appropriation of the temporal experience of the Lebenswelt is corporeally grounded in the patterned sonority of the prose rhythm which is intentionally operative in relation to his particular intentionality with regard to inhabiting the narrative perspective of particular activity. It is this perspective which is the 'position' of the 'who' of the narrative, the narrative identity.

Notes

1. See *The Fundamental Question of Metaphysics*, Chapter 1, 'An Introduction to Metaphysics'.
2. See Chapter 4, *Being and Time*.
3. It is a dilemma that Derrida seeks to avoid by means of deconstruction, and Ricoeur by a dialectic of suspicion and affirmation.
4. But Heidegger's aim is not to question in terms of the subject–predicate analytical process, since this approach assumes the ontological question to be invalid. Consequently, his attempt to question radically the 'who' disclosed in self-consciousness through the mediation of reflection is in existential terms. But this 'labour of language' may be judged a failure, particularly in the light of Derrida's critical observation with respect to the 'we' of the text.
5. The critical question is, can existential analysis escape the inherent problem of the reflective mode of being? that is, the problem of an unquestioned mode of being as the foundation for reflection. It would seem significant that existential philosophers, particularly Kierkegaard and Sartre, have written so extensively in narrative form.
6. See *The Rule of Metaphor*, p. 313.
7. This ontological understanding of textual sonority and phonicity is not to be confused with sound patterns in language related to generative phonology described in *The Sound Pattern of English*, by Noam Chomsky and Morris Halle.
8. For an interesting and valuable analysis of phenomenological intentionality with respect to rhythm, which will become a key feature of this study, see §A 'Rhythmizing Intentionality', *Rhythms* by Nicholas Abrahams.
9. Merleau-Ponty writes about music and language in 'The Intertwining – The Chiasm' and describes such moments of intensity as follows: 'We do not possess the musical or sensible ideas, precisely because they are negativity or absence circumscribed; they possess us. The performer is no longer producing or reproducing the sonata: he feels himself, and the others feel him to be at the service of the sonata; the sonata sings through him or cries out suddenly that he must "dash the bow" to follow it. And these open vortexes in the sonorous world finally form one sole vortex in which ideas fit with one another.' *The Visible and the Invisible*, p. 151.
10. 'It confirms my working hypothesis that the distinction between selfhood and sameness does not simply concern two constellations of meaning but involves two modes of being.' *Oneself as Another*, p. 309.
11. See 'The Hermeneutical Imagination' in Richard Kearney's *Poetics of Imagining*.
12. This hidden power of interrogation will be looked at more closely in relation to Ricoeur's notion of *distanciation*. See 'The Hermeneutical Function of Distanciation' in *Hermeneutics & the Social Sciences*. See also 'Philosophical Interrogation' in Merleau-Ponty's *The Visible and the Invisible*. The notion of interrogation has its roots in Aristotle's fundamental conviction 'All men by nature desire to know', *Metaphysics* 1.1, 980a21. See also Jonathan Lear's *Aristotle the Desire to Understand*, chapter 1.
13. See 'Resonance' in R.L. Trask's *A Dictionary of Phonetics and Phonology*, particularly with respect to 'resonant frequencies'. See also Merleau-Ponty's *The Visible and the Invisible*, p. 133ff, beginning, 'The look, we said envelops, palpates, espouses the visible things. As though it were in a relation of a pre-

established harmony with them ...'. Another interesting literary source, with respect to involuntary memory, is to be found in Marcel Proust's *Remembrance of Things Past*, particularly in the concluding part *Time Regained* in Vol. 3.

14. See *A History of Reading* by Alberto Manguel, particularly 'Learning to Read'.
15. See *Mimesis, Culture, Art, Society*, tr. Don Reneau.
16. *Phrasikleia: An Anthropology of Reading in Ancient Greece*, tr. Janet Lloyd.
17. See 'The Rhythm of Continuity: Prose' in *An Anatomy of Criticism*, pp. 263–8.
18. *Ethos* see Aristotle's *Poetics*, chapter xv, and *dianoia* see chapter xix. For a helpful discussion see the Critical Notes in S.H. Butcher's translation, p. 337ff.
19. See *Poetics*, vi. 1450a.7; *mythos* – plot, *ethos* – character, *dianoia* – thought, *melos* – analogous or otherwise connected to music, *lexis* – diction, *opsis* – spectacle.
20. See *Anatomy of Criticism*, pp. 243–4.
21. See note 20.
22. Although Nicholas Abraham's *Rhythms* deals mainly with poetic rhythm, it offers a valuable analysis which may be related to *prose rhythm*. See the first part, 'Outline of a Phenomenology of Poetic Expression', particularly the Semantic and Mythological layers.
23. See Nicholas Abraham's *Rhythms* with respect to his notion of *Paradeictic* as related to translation pp. 133–54.
24. See 'Proust and Signs': 'Proust's work is based not on exposition of memory, but on the apprenticeship of signs' (p. 4). Quoted by Ricoeur in *Time and Narrative*, Vol. 2, p. 131.
25. See *Phenomenology of Perception*, pp. 384ff.
26. Ibid. 'The theory of the body is already a theory of perception', pp. 203–6.
27. See chapter 4, *The Visible and the Invisible*.
28. *Phenomenology of Perception*, pp. 193ff.
29. See the chapter on the Phenomenology of Language in *Signs*, pp. 88–9.
30. 'Being is the 'place' where 'modes of consciousness' are inscribed as structurations of Being (a way of thinking oneself within a society is implied in its social structure), and where structurations of Being are modes of consciousness.' *The Visible and the Invisible*, p. 253.
31. See *Phenomenology of Perception*, p. 429.
32. This understanding of metaphor relates to the sensual plasticity of the poetic mode of language together with its centripetal dynamic particularly as defined by Northrop Frye in chapter 3 of *The Great Code*.
33. See *D.H. Lawrence: Novelist* by F.R. Leavis, and *D.H. Lawrence* by Tony Slade.
34. Tony Slade's *D.H. Lawrence*, p. 63.
35. See 'Narrative Identity and the Dialectic of Selfhood and Sameness' in *Oneself as Another*, pp. 140ff. Also,'Life in Quest of a Narrative' in *On Paul Ricoeur: Narrative and Interpretation*.
36. Aristotle's *Poetics*, 1459a3–8.
37. See note 29, Chapter 2.
38. See Preface to *Phenomenology of Perception*.

Chapter 5

The Primordial Dialectic and
Temporal Perspective

Sonorous Being and the Primordial Dialectic

The act of reading a narrative involves an appropriation of the temporal perspective, being the implicit or explicit viewpoint of the 'implied author'[1] which precipitates a dialectical relationship with an interrogative stance of the Self. The reader's imaginative habitation of the narrative's *Lebenswelt* provides the temporal 'space' for a critical stance of the Self in terms of who, why, where, how, when and what. Since the Self brings to this imaginative world its own identity, the critical stance becomes a process of self-reflection.[2] Reading a story can and does change a person's self-identity through a dialectical relationship between the appropriation of the temporal perspective of the 'implied author', the narrative's identity, the 'who' or Other of the text, and self-reflection arising from the interrogative stance. Since the former calls for a letting go of Self identity in an appropriation of the identity of the Other through openness, trust and risk[3] it has a propensity towards affirmation of the latter's identity; whereas, the interrogative stance, based upon unresolved questioning, has the propensity towards suspicion of identity per se. The primordial dialectic is therefore between affirmation and suspicion, between Other and Self. What follows is an analysis of this primordial dialectic.

Temporal Perspective: Prose and Poetic Rhythm

The basis of this analysis is the act of configuration as the temporal perspective of the Other of the narrative in terms of narrative identity. I will draw upon Ricoeur's theory of narrative in volume 1 of his *Time and Narrative*, and his further work on narrative identity in *The Self as Another*, taking his three stages of *mimêsis1*, *mimêsis2* and *mimêsis3*, that is, figuration, configuration and re-figuration, as the structure of this analysis. My aim is to show how the temporal perspectival understanding, grounded in an ontological unity of Sonorous Being in relation to the primordial dialectic, creates the temporal 'space' for rational interrogation and explanation.

A critical characteristic of this hermeneutical process is the relationship of prose rhythm to the configuration of narrative. It is in the poetic mode of the text, as defined by Ricoeur, this fundamental characteristic can be seen to embrace a spectrum including poetry and narrative.[4] There is a difference between these but it is not radical, even with regard to 'rhythm'. The rhythms of poetry may be defined, phenomenlogically, in terms of particular intentionality and, within the spectrum of the poetic mode, critically relates to prose rhythm defined in terms of operative intentionality. With respect to the temporal perspective of narrative, and the spectrum of textual rhythm the reader's particular attention is rhythmically grasped by the iconic moments of metaphor against a background of prose rhythm 'operative' at the 'edge' of her consciousness.

Rhythm, in general terms, is defined as the sonorous rise and fall of words and phrases caused by the alternation of accented, or stressed, and unaccented syllables. The analogous relationship with music and dancing reveals a significant influence upon the mind and body by the effect of a regular beat. It is the regularity of the beat which determines its corporeal effect. I.A. Richards writes,

> Rhythm and its specialized form, metre, depend upon repetition, and expectancy. Equally where it fails, all rhythmical and metrical effects spring from anticipation. As a rule anticipation is unconscious. Sequences of all syllables both sounds and as images of speech-movements leave the mind ready for certain further consequences rather than others. Our momentary organization is adapted to one range of possible stimuli rather to another.
> (*Principles of Literary Criticism*, p. 103)

The importance of Richards's view is the grounding of the anticipation of rhythmic beat in the physical body. There is an expectancy of an ordered effect of sonorous patterns in the objective 'flesh'.[5] Richards writes, for example, about the understanding of metre:

> We shall never understand metre so long as we ask, 'Why does temporal pattern so excite us'? and fail to realize that the pattern itself is a vast cyclic agitation spreading all over the body, a tide of excitement pouring through the channels of the mind.
> (*Ibid.*, p. 107)

An ontological propensity towards unity is revealed in the physical resonance and activity of the body in relation to its evident anticipation of a sonorous rhythmic order.

Poetic Rhythm: Regular Beat

Traditional nursery rhymes, such as the *Mother Goose* collection are based upon patterns of sound that have a greater mnemonic role than the visual images or meaning. Every child learns *Jack and Jill, Baa, Baa, Black Sheep,*

Little Boy Blue, etc., by an mnemonic anticipation of the sound which resonates in the physical body. It is the physical ordered beat of nursery rhymes that objectively manifest an ontological grounding of a propensity towards unity. The 'flesh' resonates in anticipation of rhythmic order that is not grounded only in consciousness but the physical body.

In more developed forms of poetry, this primitive, or rather primordial, grounding is discerned in the complexity of metrical forms, which is not only derived from more sophisticated rhythmic patterning, but the structuring of the linguistic mediation of emotional and imaginative expression. The mnemonic characteristic of the rhythm is combined with feeling and visual response. For example, the use of the iambic pentameter in Gray's *Elegy Written in a Country Churchyard* expresses the feeling of quiet and peace, as well as stimulating the images of the churchyard and countryside. But the regular iambic metre with the stress on the second syllable plays a fundamental role in this effect:

> The curfew tolls the knell of parting day,
> The lowing herd winds slowly o'er the lea,
> The ploughman homeward plods his weary way
> And leaves the world to darkness and to me.

A variety of traditional metric forms including the *trochaic, dactylic* and *anapaestic* in addition to the *iambic*, each based upon two or three syllables having one stress, or accent and no more, have been used to create a range of moods and feelings grounded in an insistent regular beat. An example of the trochaic form, based upon two syllables with the stress on the first, is Charles Wolfe's *The Burial of Sir John Moore*,

> Not a drum was heard, not a funeral note,
> As his corse to the ramparts we hurried;
> Not a soldier discharged his farewell shot
> O'er the grave where our hero we buried.

The regular trochaic beat conveys a mood of solemnity combined with the sense of the slow march of the soldiers.

These are of course examples of a fixed rhythm that is held, with slight variations, throughout the poems. They are frequently also combined with a regular abab rhyming structure.[6] In the long development of poetic rhythm, the regularity often becomes more complex and subtle in not only the rhythmic patterns and rhyme structure, but the verse forms and also the use of alliteration, assonance, dissonance, onomatopoeia and other poetic techniques. Although in some poems, particularly the modern development of *vers libre*,[7] it may be difficult at first reading to discern the regular rhythmic pattern, it is a fundamental characteristic of all poetry. For example, the enormously complex structure of T.S. Eliot's *Four Quartets* is based upon a symphonic structure.[8]

In the longstanding debate regarding the difference between poetry and prose, a central issue is the part played by rhythm in each. With regard to anticipation and expectancy arising from rhythm, I.A. Richards writes,

> Both prose and verse vary immensely in the extent to which they excite this 'getting ready' process, and in the narrowness of the anticipation which is formed. Prose on the whole, with the rare exceptions of a Landor, a De Quincy, or a Ruskin, is accompanied by a very much vaguer and more indeterminate expectancy than verse. In such prose as this page, for example, little more than a preparedness for further words not all exactly alike in sound and with abstract polysyllables preponderating is all that arises. In short, the sensory or formal effect of words has very little play in the literature of analysis and exposition. But as soon as prose becomes more emotive than scientific, the formal side becomes prominent.
> (*Op. cit.*, pp. 103–4)

In other words, as soon as prose becomes, *inter alia*, narrative and not rational, abstract discourse, anticipation and expectancy become effective arising from a rhythmic pattern.

Difference between Poetic and Prose Rhythm?

The difference between poetry and prose is made more questionable in the developments of poetic forms that appear to obscure the distinction. The early appearance of blank verse, particularly in the Shakespearean dramatic form, may convey the impression that although the author's intention is to heighten human experience, particularly with respect to passion and the emotions, within the structure of the plot, and theatrical performance, the aim is also to capture the speech expressions and rhythms of commonplace, prosaic language. Such an impression, of course, fails to discern the rhythmic iambic pentameter of blank verse which would seem to separate it from prose form. Certain poets have, nevertheless, made explicit an intention to combine the poetic form with ordinary speech. Wordsworth, rejecting the stylized, classical forms of the eighteenth century in such poets as Dryden and Pope, wrote in his Preface to the *Lyrical Ballads*,

> The principal object, then, proposed in these Poems was to choose incidents and situations from common life, and to relate or describe them, throughout, as far as was possible in a selection of language really used by men ...

And later in the Preface, in relation to the distinction between poetry and prose, particularly with respect to metre, he writes,

> I here use the word 'Poetry' (though against my own judgement) as opposed to the word Prose, and synonymous with metrical composition. But much more confusion has been introduced into criticism by this contradistinction of Poetry and Prose,

instead of the more philosophical one of Poetry and Matter of Fact, or Science. The only strict antithesis to Prose is Metre; nor is this, in truth, a strict antithesis, because lines and passages of metre so naturally occur in writing prose, that it would be scarcely possible to avoid them, even were it desirable.
(*Poetical Works*, p.736)

But Wordsworth's apparent concern to establish a close interdependence between poetry and prose is criticized by his friend. In 'Biographia Literaria', Coleridge claims that the difference lies in the combination of two conditions with respect to metrical composition in writing poetry:

First, that, as *elements* of metre owe their existence to a state of increased excitement, so the metre itself should be accompanied by the natural language of excitement. Secondly, that as these elements are formed into metre *artificially*, by a *voluntary* act, with the design and for the purpose of blending *delight* with emotion, so traces of present *volition* should throughout the metrical language be proportionately discernible.
(*Selected Poetry, Prose and Letters*, p. 278)

According to Coleridge, in poetry, there must be a partnership of a spontaneous impulse of passion and emotion, and a voluntary act of the will in the creation of the metrical form. This is not appropriate for prose which aims to fulfil a representative function of 'Good Sense'.[9]

From the perspective of Merleau-Ponty's notions of operative and particular intentionalities, the views of Wordsworth and Coleridge may be seen to be complementary not contradictory. The former is concerned to show that rhythm and metrical form may be discerned in prose, whereas the latter argues that the main purpose of poetry is a conscious act to write in metre to express the emotions of spontaneous impulse: that is, to give particular attention to the metrical form. Although, for the most part, prose composition does not consciously attend to the rhythmic structure, it may be revealed in a process of critical analysis. The qualification 'for the most part' is made particularly in relation to the traditional disciplines of 'rhetoric'. In *The Art of Rhetoric*, Aristotle writes,

The form of diction should be neither fully metrical nor completely without rhythm; the former is unconvincing (as it is thought to be artificial), and at the same time it is distracting; for it makes one expect the recurrence of a similar rhythmic pattern ... On the other hand, the rhythmless is unlimited, and the speech should be circumscribed but not by metre; for what is unbounded is unpleasant and unrecognizable. All things are bounded by number, and the number of the form of diction is rhythm, of which even metres too are divisions. So the speech must have rhythm, but not metre; otherwise it will be a poem.
(*The Art of Rhetoric*, Chapter 3.8, p. 230)

Since rhetoric is conceived by Aristotle in terms of oral persuasion, this appears to raise the question whether there is a difference between prose for the purpose of public speech, and written texts. But since sound is a key characteristic in the narrative mode of the written text, 'persuasion' may be appreciated as an important element in written prose of this mode.[10]

In the developments of poetic technique in the later nineteenth century, particularly in the work of Gerard Manley Hopkins, and in this century, experiments were made with regular and irregular patterns of stress and accent as the structure of rhythm instead of metrical forms. One important aspect of this development is the attempt to capture the prose rhythms of ordinary speech with the critical awareness that the rhythm of stress and accent seem to be basic to this natural expressive mode of language.[11] Gerard Manley Hopkins experimented with a new rhythm consciously working at a pattern of stress or accents alone, which he called 'sprung rhythm', as a counterpoint to a more conventional verse structure based upon the traditional Common English Running Rhythm. In a letter to R.W. Dixon, attempting to describe 'sprung rhythm', he writes,

> To speak shortly, it consists in scanning by accents or stresses alone, without any account of the number of syllables, so that a foot may be one strong syllable or it may be many light and one strong.
> (*Poems and Prose*, selected and ed. by W.H. Gardner, p. 187)

The flexibility and patterns of irregular stress of 'sprung rhythm' are intended to express the prose rhythms of ordinary speech. In his Preface to his Collected Poems, Hopkins writes,

> … Sprung Rhythm is the most natural of things. For … it is the rhythm of common speech and of written prose, when rhythm is perceived in them.
> (*Ibid.*, p. 11)

The qualifying clause seems to reveal a hesitation as to the extent of rhythmic structure, but the statement asserts a conviction based upon considerable study and experimentation that prose does have, at the very least, patterns of rhythm.

Increased development and experimentation, particularly following the work of T.S. Eliot, has been in the form of *vers libre*. This has ranged from Eliot's eclectic use of traditional resources within a form which Philip Hobsbaum characterizes as free blank verse based upon a definite five-stress rhythm,[12] and, quoting Paull F. Baum in *The Principles of English Versification*, to certain kinds of free verse which

> … do not aim to be more than ordinary prose printed in segments more or less closely corresponding with the phrase rhythm or normal sound rhythms of language.
> (*Metre, Rhythm and Verse Form*, p. 89)

In the development of free verse, the Bible and Elizabethan prose influenced such poets as Walt Whitman and, subsequently, D.H. Lawrence and others.[13]

This recognizable form is not syllabic, or line length, or metrical rhythm, but the rhythm of cadence and stress which relates to the feeling and activity of the poem. It excites and animates the imagery so that the reader imaginatively appropriates the concrete situation and lived moment of the poem's theme. It is a controlled rhythm in which the stressed rhythm is the focus of particular intentionality employing a variety of techniques. As Coleridge observed with respect to metrical form, the rhythm of *vers libre* based upon cadence and stress is the creation of a voluntary act with the purpose of 'blending delight with emotion'; or to stimulate a controlled and yet spontaneous emotional response, in addition to visually animating the image in a state of activity.[14]

Relationship between Poetic and Prose Rhythm in Prose

The rhythms of poetry appear in narratives as the parts of the text which may be defined in terms of particular intentionality. Metaphor, which plays a key role in poetry, is the textual rhythmic focus of particular intentionality being at the forefront of the reader's consciousness, with the rhythm of the description fading into the background at the 'edge' of consciousness. In other words, rhythm plays a key role in the expression of activity and emotion in relation to particular concrete situations in terms of 'grasping' and animating a metaphoric image, or iconic moment, and 'withdraws' to the 'edge' of consciousness in the 'distancing' of reflective consciousness in response to discursive prose; and plays a significant role in 'grasping' or emplotment,[15] to use Ricoeur's term, of narrative. For the most part, prose rhythm of the latter expresses activity and emotion in terms of mood, ambience and atmosphere.

Every narrative may be analysed with regard to rhythm based upon cadence and stress. An illuminating example is F. Scott Fitzgerald's *The Great Gatsby*. In this, the mood and atmosphere of the American rich society in the 1920s is mediated through the prose rhythm of the narrator Nick Carraway. A crucial passage is the meeting of Gatsby, a wealthy man with a mysterious and suspicious background, with Daisy, a young woman married to a rich and stupid man, who had become the impossible object of Gatsby's overpowering romantic dream.

> Gatsby, his hands still in his pocket, / was reclining against the mantelpiece / *in a strained counterfeit of perfect ease* / even of boredom. / His head leaned back so far / that it rested against the face of the defunct mantelpiece clock, / and from this position / his distraught eyes stared down at Daisy, / who was sitting, frightened but graceful, / on the edge of a stiff chair.
> (*The Great Gatsby*, p. 93 [my italics])

The passage is marked to indicate the rhythm of the concerned, empathetic observation of an aspiring but melancholic young writer living in a bored society, lacking real passion. Reading this passage, as it should normally be read, without any overt critical attention to its prose rhythm, the metaphor 'strained counterfeit' is the phrase which has rhythmic predominance. In the era of prohibition and mob gangsters, counterfeiting was widespread, and the word was part of the vernacular. In this passage, employed metaphorically, it predominates because there is a concentration upon an image actively mediating a concrete visual awareness of the essential characteristics of Gatsby, not only in the way 'counterfeit' resonates with connotations of his mansion and parties, but also the society which has corrupted him and which he hopelessly attempts to rise above. The poetic rhythm of feeling and activity in this iconic moment is reflected in the prose rhythm of the passage, and throughout the novel.

In any full analysis, it would be worthwhile making comparison with other novels. Simply to read the beginning of two or more immediately stimulates an awareness of different moods mediated through the language. It is to be aware of inhabiting different lifeworlds. For example, to compare Scott Fitzgerald's *Great Gatsby* with two other American novels, William Faulkner's *Absalom, Absalom!* and Ernest Hemingway's *Farewell to Arms*, is to be aware of the very different world of Faulkner's fictional Yoknapatawpha County in the long, lyrical sentences, and the gritty, insistent determination expressed in Hemingway's clipped, staccato, journalistic style prose.

Narrative analysis may reveal the forms of prose rhythm by focusing attention on the metaphoric features and the use of poetic techniques of various metrical forms, but particularly the cadence and stress patterns which fade into the background of mood and ambience in the discursive prose. The study of poetic techniques in terms of the poet's attempts to listen critically to the acoustics of prose informs a critical analysis of the prose rhythm of the creative writer. Narrative is the creation of form and structure in which prose rhythm plays a key role in terms of ontological grounding.

Rhythm and Temporality

Returning now to the fundamental issue of the claim made by I.A. Richards that anticipation and expectancy are the effects of the regular beat or stress; and the effects of bodily activity or resonance. Phenomenologically, the rhythm is mediated in terms of feeling and activity in relation to figuration. What does this mean? Anticipation and expectancy are the mediation of temporality; and feeling and activity in relation to narrative take place in 'human' time. Rhythm is the mediation of the Heideggerian triadic 'ekstases' of coming-to-be, having-been and being present. Heidegger's anticipatory resoluteness in the face of being-towards-death is here qualified by a rhythm of hope.[16] That is, prose rhythm, in terms of the resonance of the 'flesh', is the ontological disclosure of the temporality of *Dasein*. Or, to put it another way, it is the ontological disclosure of the propensity, or dunamis, of Sonorous Being towards temporal order or unity. But such novels as Marcel Proust's *A la recherché du temps perdu*, James Joyce's *Ulysses*, and Virginia Woolf's *To the Lighthouse*, among many other modern novels which are devoted to a subjective exploration of 'human' time,[17] disclose, to use a spatial metaphor, a 'multi-dimensional' temporality which suggests a more flexible horizon of temporal being than Heidegger's triadic ekstases.

Configuration and Rhythm

The phenomenological mediation of emotion and activity is temporally structured. Emotion in terms of the expressions of hope, despair, joy, sadness, anxiety, peace, frustration, satisfaction, and activity perceived as image and figure, in terms of narrative, are clearly set within 'human' time. There are implicit, if not explicit, temporal horizons for all emotion and activity as part of narrative. They are grounded in anticipation and expectancy of the 'flesh' as the mediation of Sonorous Being. The act of 'grasping' the narrative by means of its temporal perspective is therefore the act of configuring the linguistic mediation of emotion and activity grounded in the ontological sonority of prose rhythm. This is a fundamental issue between Kant's notion of the productive imagination and the act of configuration with respect to Ricoeur's notion of emplotment: that is, the issue of an ontological grounding, in contrast to a transcendental understanding, of the productive imagination and act of configuration. However, although Ricoeur's analysis of configuration attempts to ground this act in the symbolic structuring, he does not give enough attention to phonicity, and consequently is lacking in a clear understanding of the ontological foundation of this act.[18] He places considerable emphasis upon the ability to follow a story which seems to imply that this ability is grounded in a transcendental, phenomenological act of perception. Although this conclusion does not take account of Ricoeur's notion of narrative identity and ontological view set out in the tenth study of *Oneself as Another*, by which he seems to escape the accusation of transcendental subjectivism, there are critical ontological questions which can only be resolved by the role played by prose rhythm.

Practical Field of Human Experience

Ricoeur defines the ontological grounding of the act of configuration in terms of three features: structural, symbolic and temporal. The first feature is based upon an understanding of the way action is given meaning in relation to a whole conceptual network which is paradigmatic with respect to the regular and familiar patterns of human activity. There is a linguistic prefiguration which Ricoeur claims potentially and actually gives rise to the syntagmatic order of narrated discourse; all actions have agents which are subject to the questions about 'what,' 'why', 'who', 'how', 'with whom', or 'against whom'.[19] This gives a temporal character to the linguistic network or texture which may be compared with Merleau-Ponty's notion of *Prose of the World*. He writes,

> Speech always comes into play against the background of speech; it is always only a fold in the immense fabric of language. To understand it, we do not have to consult some inner lexicon which gives us pure thoughts covered up by words or forms we are perceiving; we have only to lend ourselves to its life, to its movement of differentiation and articulation, and to its eloquent gestures.
> ('Indirect Language and the Voices of Silence', *Signs*, p. 42)

The pressing question is, however, what is the ontological characteristic of this anchorage in the practical field of temporal existence? What Ricoeur and Merleau-Ponty seem to describe is the phenomenological characteristics of the linguistic network or sedimentation in which narrative discourse is rooted.

The second anchorage of configuration is the symbolic resources of this field. Drawing upon the work of Ernst Cassirer, in his *Philosophy of Symbolic Forms*,[20] Ricoeur agrees that symbolic forms are cultural processes that articulate experience. That is, symbols underlie human action and constitute its first signification before symbolic wholes become detached through speech and writing. This understanding of symbols moves the analysis closer to an ontological viewpoint. Symbols are not in the mind but are incorporated into action which is consequently decipherable, or readable by other actors in the social interplay.

The objective nature of Ricoeur's definition of symbols was considered in Chapter 2 with respect to the iconic moment of metaphor. But, as was noted, he does not pursue the sonorous characteristic of this iconic moment, and therefore fails to take account of its ontological implications.

Rhythm and the Field of Human Experience

The rhythmic pattern of this sonority in relation to the structure of the linguistic conceptual network, or Prose of the World, and the texture of symbolic mediation, is the ontological manifestation of their grounding in Sonorous Being, or Prose Rhythm of the World. Prose rhythm is the ontological centripetal dynamic of symbolic mediation, and narrative configuration. In this sense, action not only gives rise, through human competence of signification, to conceptual networks, and the symbolic texture of mediation, but resonates with rhythm that is integrally part of these networks and texture.

It is also significant that certain rhythmic patterns of human action are related to the seasons, to day and night, and other terrestial rhythms which influence and shape the rhythms of temporal existence. Also, the corporeal rhythms of breathing and cardiac pulsation directly relate to the patterns of human activity. Ritual acts and social patterns of behaviour are permeated with rhythm which is the anchorage of linguistic prose rhythm in the practical field of temporal existence, and are the manifestation of the ontological grounding of the conceptual networks and symbolic texture which underlie narrative configuration.

Corporeal rhythm is phenomologically disclosed in sound and sight. Bodily rhythm is expressed in sound patterns and figuration. This is evident in ritual acts in the part played by music and symbolic figuration. In dance, the body not only expresses the musical rhythms but is expressed by them. So too, bodily rhythm is expressed in the figuration of dance. The phenomenological disclosure of corporeal rhythm gives meaning to the behavioural patterns of the practical field of human experience, and the cultural configuration of a Lebenswelt, and the anchorage of the linguistic phonic gestures in prose rhythm.

Ontological Disclosure

But does this mean that it is only in this disclosure that the ontological nature of prose rhythm is made known? If so, is it speculative to propose that prose rhythm is the ontological manifestation of Sonorous Being? Consequently, does the transcendental subject remain to confound the analysis? Is all phenomenological disclosure subject to intentionality and the Self's rational attempt to wrest the appearance from the Other and enfold it in the realm of the Same? But if, for example, the figure does indeed appear, is it possible to trace its contours as the structuralist attempts to do in the realm of the Same?

If configuration is indeed understood as an ontological disclosure, if narrative configuration is the appropriation of a lifeworld, an active condition of being-in-the-world, what is the nature of this disclosure as an act of appropriation? If the ontological disclosure of being is the *figure* (*Gestalt*), what is the nature of this phenomenological disclosure by which it is not ensnared in the realm of the Same? To put it another way, is it possible for the figure to be both present and absent? For example, is it possible for the figure of the iconic moment of metaphor to be subject to particular intentionality and yet to lie beyond its attention? Is it possible that any attempt to trace the contour of the figure is an illusion? And yet, the figure appears! Or, is it that which is circumscribed by the figure that appears? For example, the profile of a three-dimensional figure is never the line of the contour. Because the visual appearance is only possible from one of an infinite possibility of perspectives, the contour of any profile is an abstraction, and the figure never appears. And yet, that which is circumscribed by the elusive figure does appear. It is partial, and may seemingly be distorted, but it appears as the effect of the centripetal dynamic of the figure. If temporality and activity are added to this three-dimensional figure, the dynamic of the figure is the rhythmic resonance as the effect of Sonorous Being. In this sense, the figure is both present and absent, it invokes affirmation and suspicion.

The act of appropriation of a narrative is the 'grasping' of the configuration of the Lebenswelt, the 'bringing together', the con-figuring of the totality of narrative's temporal activity in terms of its characters and events. Appropriation is the relationship of particular and operative intentionalities which resonate with poetic and prose rhythm. Prose rhythm is at the edge of consciousness and beyond. Configuration is both present and absent. It invokes affirmation of narrative unity, but also suspicion because any attempt to abstract the configuration as a way of explaining the lifeworld, or any feature of it, must remain open to endless interpretation. Appropriation is the possibility of affirming narrative unity, or identity, as the mediation of the Other, in a dialectical relationship with reflection, in terms of a continuing provocation of Self reflection in the realm of the Same.[21]

Narrative Configuration

Martha Nussbaum provides a valuable interpretation of the act of appropriation, of 'grasping' a narrative configuration in her essays on philosophy and literature under the title *Love's Knowledge*. One of her aims is to demonstrate the importance of literature as a source of moral understanding. In the creative act of the writer, where moral issues are at stake, according to Nussbaum, these are informed by a moral vision that gives unity to the complex and subtle multi- faceted characteristics and features of the characters and events of the narrative. Consequently, moral issues are not resolved into a set of dicta or clearly defined principles, but are 'grasped' in a configuration whereby a process of 'open' reflection may be conducted. In other words, moral vision is affirmed at the same time that the attempt to complete moral definitions is held under suspicion. Nussbaum takes the novels of Henry James, in particular *The Golden Bowl*, and proposes that the entire novel is given moral significance and unity in a passage taken from Chapter III of Book Five, in which the father of Maggie makes an act of sacrifice in giving her up so that she is free to love her husband. It is the complete image of this passage which evokes a profound sense of moral achievement in configuring the complete narrative of the novel. She writes,

> We can say several things about the moral significance of this picture. First, that as a picture it is significant – not only in its causal relation to his subsequent speeches and acts, but as a moral achievement in its own right. It is, of course, of enormous causal significance; his speeches and acts, here and later, flow forth from it and take from it the rightness of their tone ... Furthermore, the picture has a pivotal role in his moral activity here that would not be captured by regarding it as a mere precondition for action. We want to say, *here* is where his sacrifice, his essential

moral choice, takes place ... here James tells us that sacrifice is an act of imaginative interpretation.
(*Love's Knowledge*, p. 151–2)

According to Nussbaum, this moral achievement cannot be captured in paraphrase; it is not, as it were, a two-dimensional definition, or even description, of conceptual morality. It is a work of art.

> It is seeing a complex, concrete reality in a highly lucid and richly responsive way; it is taking in what there is there, with imagination and feeling.
> (*Ibid.*, p. 152)

Although she does not explore in detail the importance of prose rhythm, she does make a significant and important comment in comparing the original prose with a paraphrase which

> ... even when reasonably accurate, does not ever succeed in displacing the original prose; for it is, not being a high work of literary art, devoid of richness of feeling and a rightness of tone and rhythm that characterize the original, whose cadences stamp themselves inexorably on the heart.
> (*Ibid.*, p. 154)

It is the unity of the creative act of imagination in configuring the text which can only be responded by inhabiting the prose rhythm of the text. To be captured by the image, to visualize the moral achievement, or to discern that which lies beyond this achievement in terms of the unity, the identity of the narrative, is to inhabit a corporeal resonance which is not present, that is, does not appear, with respect to reflection in the realm of the Same, but makes present that which is circumscribed by the configuration.

The unity of this vision is not threatened by an apparent destruction of any hope of ultimate rational resolution. When captured by the unity of the vision there may seem to be a profound sense of rational affirmation in spite of an endless provocation of the open horizon. The quality of the father's sacrifice in the passage from *The Golden Bowl* as the key image of the entire novel does appear to make sense. It gives meaning to the narrative which does not seem to deny a rational explanation of the story even though any such explanation must be subject to continuing reinterpretation.

Notes

1. See *Time and Narrative*, Vol. 3, pp. 160–66. Also Martha Nussbaum's distinction of three author figures in *Love's Knowledge*, pp. 9–10. A useful definition may be found in Jeremy Hawthorn's *A Concise Glossary of Contemporary Literary Theory*, under the entry, 'Author', pp. 11–12.
2. This process is central to hermeneutical philosophy. For example, see 'Analysis of Historically Effected Consciousness' in Gadamer's *Truth and Method*, pp.

341ff. With particular regard to Ricoeur's thought, the essay by Kathleen Blamey, 'From the Ego to the Self' in *The Philosophy of Paul Ricoeur*, ed. L.E. Hahn, is of interest and importance.

3. The notion of risk is an existential one with respect to the security of self-identity. It relates to Kierkegaard's understanding of becoming a Christian, see *The Journal's of Kierkegaard*, pp. 185–6; also to his *Concept of Dread*, and the notion of 'the leap' of faith.

4. Ricoeur draws upon Aristotle's *Poetics* and the 'all-emcompassing concept' of *mimesis*. See *Time and Narrative*, Vol. 1, p. 33ff.

5. See Merleau-Ponty's *The Visible and the Invisible* pp. 248–51.

6. For a brief outline of rhyme structure see chapter 4 of Philip Hobsbaum's *Metre, Rhythm and Verse Form*.

7. *Ibid.*, chapter 7.

8. See Eliot's essay, 'The Music of Poetry' in *On Poetry and Poets*, particularly, '... there are possibilities of transitions in a poem comparable to the different movements of a symphony or a quartet.' p. 38.

9. *Biographia Literaria*, p. 270.

10. For an examination of the influence of ancient oratory and rhetoric upon literary genres see *Persuasion: Greek Rhetoric in Action*, ed. Ian Worthington. See also *The Bible as Rhetoric*, ed. Martin Warner.

11. See entries under 'stress' in *A Dictionary of Phonetics and Phonology*, by R.L. Trask.

12. *Metre, Rhythm and Verse Form*, p. 96.

13. *Ibid.*, pp. 100–10.

14. See Northrop Frye's *Anatomy of Criticism*, pp. 243–4.

15. See *Time and Narrative*, vol. 1, chapter 2.

16. In his critique of Heidegger in *Time and Narrative*, vol. 3, p. 78, Ricoeur writes, 'What appears to me to be shunted aside is the problematic of the trace ...'. This comment is made in reference to the past. It also may be made with respect to the future in terms of the sonorous mediation of the trace as rhythms of hope.

17. See chapter 3, 'Time' in *Modernist Fiction* by Randall Stevenson.

18. In *Time and Narrative*, vol.1, p. 32ff, Ricoeur gives some thought to melody in Aristotle's *Poetics* with respect to imitation, and also the notions of concordance and discordance. But he does not appear to pursue the musical connotations of these notions in terms of phonicity and the ontological possibilities. In *The Rule of Metaphor* he makes clear his understanding of the work of resemblance involves an auditory characteristic in terms of the sensible characteristic of poetic language (p. 209), but does not develop the critical ontological implications as presented in this study.

19. See *ibid.*, pp. 54–7.

20. See *Freud & Philosophy*, pp. 10–11.

21. See, 'Textuality and the Question of Origin: Heidegger's reading of "Andenken" and "Der Ister"' in *Heidegger and the Poets*, Véronique M. Fóti.

22. They are aesthetic creations that may be considered analogous to music. See George Steiner's *Real Presences*, particularly pp. 215–27.

Chapter 6

Self and Other

Abraham's Sacrifice

Tragedies, and those narratives which seem to present an absurd challenge to reason, raise the issue of the relationship between suspicion and affirmation in its most acute form. The biblical story of Abraham's sacrifice of Isaac (see Appendix) is an example of the latter. But an analysis of its prose rhythm in a particular text reveals that it is possible to understand this seemingly incomprehensible act in a way that opens up a hermeneutical process in terms of rational probabilities; that is, an understanding achieved by an openness to meaning, unconstrained by the semantic past, which vehemently provokes rational explanation into securing innovative probabilities. It is the question of grasping the singularity of an act not by means of universal conceptuality but by the mediation of a configuration which acts as a schema for the conceptual manifold.[1]

Literary Approach to the Text

I will treat the biblical narrative as a story free from any theological presuppositions or exegetical purposes with respect to a community of religious faith, and not address any historical or anthropological issues such as child sacrifice. Although the text is an integral part of the Biblical written tradition that has been subjected to seemingly considerable redaction, which in turn has inspired a critical hermeneutical process drawing upon wide-ranging studies of archaeological, anthropological and other disciplines, it is the story as preserved in a particular text that I will analyse. What is at stake is the process of inhabiting the lifeworld of the text in terms of appropriating the ontological perspective of the Other of the narrative whereby the meaning of the story may be understood, provoking uninhibited attempts at rational explanation.

Prose rhythm is a key characteristic of such appropriation, and therefore my analysis is limited to a particular text in a particular language and a particular translation. It is not a question of whether a particular translation accurately mediates the original text; it is an ontological issue of habitation involving fundamental acoustical and visual characteristics that are peculiar to the prose rhythm of a particular linguistic form of the narrative.

'Authorized Version' of the Biblical Text

The particular text I have selected is the 'Authorized Version' of the Bible
first published in 1611 and dedicated to King James. Although its accuracy as
a translation of the original Hebrew and Greek has been criticized, it is
commended for sharing the simple, concrete and direct characteristics of the
Hebrew language.[2] According to a number of scholars of the English
language, these characteristics have informed and influenced its development
in literature and the vernacular. For example, Addison wrote,

> There is a certain coldness and indifference in the phrases of our European
> languages, when compared with the oriental forms of speech; and it happens very
> luckily, that the Hebrew idioms run into the English tongue with a particular grace
> and beauty. Our language has received innumerable elegancies and improvements,
> from that infusion of Hebraism, which are derived to it out of the poetical passages
> in Holy Writ. They give force and energy to our expression, warm and animate our
> language, and convey our thoughts in more ardent and intense phrases, than any
> that are to be met with in our own tongue.
> (*'Spectator'*, No. 405 quoted in T.R. Henn's *The Bible as Literature*, p. 35)

T.R. Henn also refers to the cadence, favoured by the translators, as the
metrical pattern marking the final clauses of sentences in certain kinds of
prose.[3] He notes the way this Hebraic aspect has been taken up into the
'Authorized Version' of the Bible in its development in the English language:

> It passes into English through late Latin, and particularly through the rhythms of
> the Cranmer prayer- book, deriving from the Mass. It appears strongly in the Latin
> versions of the Psalms, and widely dispersed, in the Latin of St. Jerome's Vulgate
> which was so familiar to the early Translators.
> (*The Bible as Literature*, p. 39)

Writing in Peake's Commentary on the Bible, he expresses the view that

> It seems probable that its rhythms are embedded in us (first through the Latin of
> ritual, and their transpositions into English Liturgy) so firmly as to condition our
> recognition, and response to, all other rhythms of a similar nature.
> (*Peake's Commentary*, p. 8)

It is evident that the 'Authorized Version' was the climax of a number of
Biblical translations in the age of the Renaissance, 1500 to 1650, which
played a significant role in linguistic development of what has become known
as the Modern English Period.[4] In their *The History of the English Language*,
Albert C. Baugh and Thomas Cable outline the important and key
developments which established the Modern period, for example, in
vocabulary, grammar and pronunciation, particularly vowel sounds,
maintaining a continuity of characteristics in the constant changes of
historical development.

The point I am making is that the sedimentations of present-day English may not only be identified in the conventional meaning of words and idioms, but also in the rhythms traced to the Renaissance in which the 'Authorized Version' of the Bible is a crucial influence. Consequently, the resonance and sonority which play an important role in the appropriation of English prose narratives may be, directly or indirectly, regulated by the Biblical rhythms – a regulation that may be understood as a key characteristic of the ontological sonorous condition of those for whom English is indigenous to their native lifeworld.

The Problem in Understanding the Narrative

In Genesis chapter 22, verses 1 to 19, it is clear that the difficulty in understanding lies in Abraham's seeming willingness to sacrifice his son. It is in the relationship of verse 10, with its succinct description of taking the knife to slay Isaac, and verse 2, which states without reservation, in the words of God, the love of Abraham for his son, that any attempt to understand the narrative is given its sharpest challenge. Although it may be helpful to have some knowledge of the larger Genesis narrative of which this sacrifice is part, including the expressions of Abraham's faith and obedience, and the divine blessings he and his wife, Sarah, receive, especially the gift of a son in their old age, these do not detract from the profound difficulty of understanding the relationship between verses 2 and 10. There may be the temptation to suggest that Abraham believed that God would withhold his hand at the last moment and provide for the sacrifice. Since this is indeed what happens in verse 11 and following, and since Abraham had experienced God's blessings in the past, the greatest being the gift of Isaac, it may seem reasonable to explain verse 10 in this way. But there is no basis for this interpretation in verses 1 to 10. Furthermore, if Abraham does have this belief, the act itself does not make sense. The narrative of God's tempting Abraham must surely mean that he cannot stretch forth his hand to slay his son unless he is willing to perform the act. What is so seemingly incomprehensible in this narrative is not, primarily, the ways of God, nor any metaphysical speculation about the existence or nature of the Divinity, or the covenantal relationship between the Hebrew Deity and the Father of its Faith, but the motive of an old man in the act of sacrificing his son.[5] How is it possible to appropriate and inhabit the lifeworld of this old man to begin to understand and make sense of this act?

Configuration and Metaphor

In Chapter 3 I have shown that if the narrative is to be rationally understood and open to explanation, there must be access to its narrative identity in terms of the perspective of its 'implied author', that is, to be critically aware of the focus of configuration which dynamically draws together the total figuration of the narrative. If there is such a perspective it must surely be centred upon the moment of the act in verse 10: 'And Abraham stretched forth his hand, and took the knife to slay him.' It is in the figure of this direct, pithy description that the reader's imagination is given a viewpoint, a *gestalt* whereby his particular and operative intentionalities are configured. The various figures leading to this key moment are formed in relation to the sacrificial act. For example, the imaginative perception of Abraham rising early in the morning saddling his ass, capturing every feature and characteristic of his movements and bodily expression, is informed by the impending moment when he stretches forth his hand to strike with the knife. The significant aspect of this configuration is the interrelationship of the figure in verse 10 with the figure of a loving father mediated by the words in verse 2, 'Take thy son, thine only son Isaac, whom thou lovest …'. What is the imaginative perception of this figure from the perspective of the Other of the text?

A closer examination of the relationship between verses 2 and 10 reveals that it involves more than an act of configuration. From Ricoeur's work on semantic innovation in which there is a close relationship between his theories of narrative and metaphor, the figure in verse 10 may be seen not only as the focus of the configuration but also the iconic moment in a metaphor which is integrally related to the emplotment of the narrative. In other words, the iconic moment is the symbolic mediation which precipitates a semantic interactive process throughout the discourse, or narrative. It is an act of appropriation and habitation with respect to a metaphor which involves semantic innovation born out of interaction.[6]

I am proposing that the biblical story of Abraham's sacrifice in Genesis chapter 22 may, and indeed should, be read as a metaphor. Therefore, to begin to understand and explain this seemingly incomprehensible narrative calls for an act of configuration involving a response to the symbolic mediation of the metaphor. The key figure of configuration, and the iconic moment of the metaphor is verse 10, 'And Abraham stretched forth his hand, and took the knife to slay his son.' The cultic act of sacrifice is symbolic;[7] the meaning is a 'this for that'. But the act does not stand for something else. The literal meaning as set out in verse 10 is taken up and transcended by a new meaning created out of an interaction between verse 10 and the rest of the narrative, particularly verse 2. It may be helpful to have some understanding of the cultic practice of sacrifice, but it is clear in the text alone that the act of sacrifice in verse 10 is symbolic, and, in terms of the literary characteristics of the narrative, it is a metaphor.

To begin to understand the act involves grasping its figuration, to imaginatively perceive this moment from the narrative's perspective. Consequently, the figure cannot be grasped on the basis of a literal understanding. The figure takes on a symbolic aspect which mediates a revealed, or rather created, meaning since the reader's imagination is involved in a creative process in the rest of the text. Therefore, as a result of the appropriation and habitation of the narrative's ontological viewpoint, the perspective of the Other, the literal meaning of 'And Abraham stretched forth his hand, and took the knife to slay his son' vehemently interacts in the semantic field of the narrative, particularly with verse 2a, 'And he said, Take now thy son, thine only son Isaac, whom thou lovest, and get thee into the land of Moriah'. The meaning of the sacrifice may only be understood in terms of the imaginative visual appropriation of the figure of Abraham as the loving father of Isaac. A superficial attempt to understand could be that the meaning of this sacrifice is Abraham's decision to give up the one who is most precious to him. But if Abraham's love for Isaac is completely selfless, then this meaning of the act would not be rational, it would be paradoxically selfish, since giving up in this way would be satisfying Abraham's personal faith and conviction. In other words, he would be willing to kill his son in order to maintain his own existential security.[8]

There have been many attempts at interpretation in which the symbolic and metaphoric features have been explicitly or implicitly taken into account. For example, Gerhard von Rad makes the claim,

> There are many levels of meaning, and whoever thinks he has discovered virgin soil must discover at once that there are many more layers below that. Such a mature narrator as this one has no intention of paraphrasing exactly the meaning of such an event and stating it for the reader. On the contrary, a story like this is basically open to interpretation and to whatever thoughts the reader is inspired.
> (*Genesis, A Commentary*, p. 238)

But the critical question is, can there be any level of meaning discovered in the relationship between verses 2 and 10 in the text? In his commentary von Rad suggests,

> It has to do with a road out into God forsakenness on which Abraham does not know that God is only testing him. There is thus considerable religious experience behind these nineteen verses: that Yahweh often seems to contradict himself, that he appears to remove the salvation begun by himself from history. But in this way Yahweh tests faith and obedience!
> (*Ibid.*, p. 239)

Yet this level of meaning is grounded in metaphysical assumptions which, from a philosophical point of view, not only challenge rational explanation but act as a closure on any further attempts at interpretation.[9]

The Linguistic Mediation of Singularity

The problem in its most acute form is presented by Derrida in *The Gift of Death*. The essay in Chapter 3, 'Whom to Give to (Knowing not to Know)', takes the issue of the individual's responsibility and decision, with respect to Abraham's act of sacrifice, as a singularity which cannot be linguistically communicated, and therefore cannot be understood by others. The understanding of the decision to act is a secret between God and Abraham. He writes,

> To the extent that, in not saying the essential thing, namely, the secret between God and him, Abraham doesn't speak, he assumes the responsibility that consists in always being alone, entrenched in one's own singularity at the moment of decision. Just as no one can die in my place, no one can make a decision, what we call 'a decision,' in my place. But as soon as one speaks, as soon as one enters the medium of language, one loses that very singularity.
> (*The Gift of Death*, p. 59–60)

If Derrida is correct, then all linguistic meaning is either based upon *a priori* assumptions, or is conventional, and there is no foundation for rational affirmation other than conventionality. If it is not possible to grasp, to have some understanding of the other's singularity in the moment of decision, there is no possibility of a linguistic perspective for a hermeneutical process in which understanding constantly provokes continuing explanation. With regard to the Biblical narrative in question, from Derrida's approach, there is no possibility of understanding Abraham's decision to sacrifice his son, and therefore the story is incomprehensible.[10]

It is, however, incomprehensible only in terms of the possibility of an universal conceptuality of Abraham's singularity in the moment of decision. Derrida states,

> We would no longer dare speak of 'the universal concept of responsibility'.
> (*Ibid.*, p. 61)

There is of course such a concept, but the point that Derrida is making is that it does not communicate the singularity of the moment of decision. He does not however address the question whether it is a concept that may be subject to continuing openness of interpretation in an affirmation of unity of a rational 'space' grounded in the singularity of the moment of decision. That is, to appropriate the configuration of the narrative, and the iconic moment of the key metaphor, is to affirm an understanding that opens the rational 'space' for continual rational explanation. It is to grasp the meaning of the singularity of the moment of decision so that it may indeed be linguistically mediated in terms of rational explanation.

Self and Other

For this to be so, the reader must appropriate a condition of being by a willingness to relinquish any sense of finality of meaning. It is a question of a relationship between Self and Other whereby the Self may inhabit the Other's ontological viewpoint producing a semantic innovation in the process of self-reflection. The concept of Otherness has been the subject of considerable interest in recent philosophical debate, particularly in the work of Emmanuel Levinas. According to Levinas, there is no possibility of understanding and explaining the Other. The metaphysical absolute desire for the Other places it outside self-consciousness.[11] From this perspective, Levinas contends that the history of Western philosophy reveals the attempt of the conscious I to grasp the Other through the mediation of appearance and enfold it in the sphere of the Same in terms of rational explanation.[12] That is, the sphere of cognitive, conceptual mediation which is dependent upon repetition[13] with respect to meaning and knowledge, and the continuing identity of the self-conscious I. He writes,

> Our relation with the other (*autrui*) certainly consists in wanting to comprehend him, but this relation overflows comprehension. Not only because knowledge of the other (*autrui*) requires, outside of all curiosity, also sympathy or love, ways of being distinct from impassible contemplation, but because in our relation with the other (*autrui*), he does not affect us in terms of a concept. He is a being (*étant*) and counts as such.
> (*Basic Philosophical Writings*, 'Is Ontology Fundamental?', p. 6)

Levinas maintains that the relationship of the I with the Other is, more than anywhere else, in the face of the other human being, of the stranger. He claims that the position of the I in this relationship is not one of an awareness of duty and obligation, it is responsibility through and through. It is an ethical relationship in which the response is founded not upon comprehension but unquestionable responsibility. For this reason, he argues that metaphysics, in the sense of ethics as the First Philosophy, precedes ontology, and is therefore critical of Heidegger's attempt to comprehend Being. He writes,

> If ontology – the comprehension, the embracing of Being – is impossible, it is not because every definition of Being already presupposes the knowledge of Being, as Pascal had said and Heidegger refutes in the first pages of *Being and Time*; it is because the comprehension of Being in general cannot *dominate* the relationship with the Other. The latter relationship commands the first. I cannot disentangle myself from society with the Other, even when I consider the Being of the existent he is.
> (*Totality and Infinity*, p. 47)

There is a radical dichotomy between the Self and Other in Levinas's philosophy which cannot be bridged by any act of comprehension.

My concern is with the Other specifically as the Other of narrative, that is, the 'implied author', the ontological perspective which configures the narrative consequently structuring the rational 'space' whereby analysis and explanation may be conducted in the sphere of the Same. In contrast to

Levinas, my aim is to demonstrate that an act of comprehension may take place. This is not an Heideggerian comprehension of Being, but a comprehension grounded upon the perspective of the Being of the Other. What is comprehended is not the latter but the Other's viewpoint. The reader is called to act in a process of appropriation and habitation of the ontological position of the Other. The act does not bridge the radical dichotomy between the Self and Other in terms of comprehension; the Other still overflows comprehension in the metaphysical desire of the Self for the absolute Other. What the act does achieve is a dialectical relationship between the Self and Other in the way the appropriation of the ontological perspective of the Other vehemently provokes semantic innovation in the sphere of the Same.

Prose Rhythm and the Biblical Text

Returning to the 'Authorized Version' of the Biblical text, the prose rhythm of this text reveals the possibility of a sonorous effect which provides a dynamic vehemence in the metaphorical relationship between verses 2 and 10, whereby the iconic moment focused upon the figure of the act of sacrifice in the latter verse takes into itself the love of Abraham for Isaac in the former. This particular prose rhythm effects a bodily resonance in the act of reading that precipitates an ontological convergence in terms of an operative intentionality beyond the 'edge' of consciousness which, in the sense of Merleau-Ponty's phenomenology, makes possible an act of particular intentionality. That is, the prose rhythm of the 'Authorized Version' makes it possible to grasp the meaning of this particular act. This particular text linguistically mediates the singularity of the act in terms of a teleological, open process of rational explanation.

I have given some consideration to the prose rhythm of the 'Authorized Version' of the Bible in the way that the English reader may therefore be 'tuned' to its rhythm, comparable to the cultural indigenous patterns of musical beat which initiate an involuntary response to a rich variety of song and dance. The role of these patterns in the convergence of configurations of sound and movement in melody and motion is significant. But even if the rhythms of the 'Authorized Version' were influential in this manner, this would be a matter of conventionality. Linguistic sedimentation in itself cannot be considered as a grounding for rational affirmation. It is important nevertheless to recognize that it is an integral part of understanding and explanation and may be influential in the reader's act of appropriation and habitation.

The rhythmic patterns of stress in this Abrahamic passage, are concrete, and direct descriptions of action and place. There are few adjectives, or adverbs, or subordinate clauses. Typical of the 'Authorized Version', reflecting the original Hebrew, it has a simple conjunctive style with few connecting participles. The effect is a dramatic force carrying the narrative along, moving through peaks of action. Its simplicity of style tends to place the dominant stress pattern on the verb, focusing the reader's attention on the concrete moments of action, constraining any distraction by reflection upon the descriptive features of the characters and place. In responding to the dynamic of the direct and concrete movement of action, the reader's imagination is rooted in the characters in a state of activity. The dominant focus, and therefore rhythmic stress, is not upon their thoughts or emotions but actions. Any reflection upon the former is after the narrative has been read. Whatever meaning emerges from the act of reading is imaginatively grounded in the appropriation and habitation of the concrete actions.

It is obvious from the text that this grounding is directly related to the figure of Abraham. In the first ten verses his name is mentioned ten times. The figure dominates the whole narrative: it is the story of Abraham's sacrifice of his son. Significantly, the word 'son' is found eight times in the same verses, with the repetition in verse 2, whereas the name Isaac is found only five times. Consequently, the effect is to grasp imaginatively the figure of Abraham in action in his relationship with his son. It is the figure of the father in the act of killing his son. But this is an act of sacrifice, and the purpose, according to the narrative, is to tempt Abraham. The son, therefore, in the moment of the act is the means of this temptation. That is, the literal meaning of the son becomes the metaphoric meaning of temptation in the act of sacrifice. It is clear from the narrative that Abraham's relationship with God is being tested. The command to perform this sacrificial act is a testing of obedience. Beyond that, the nature of this obedience is speculative. What is not speculative is the objective mode of this testing in the son. The son is the objective mode of this act of testing. Therefore, the figure of the son in the act of sacrifice is a metaphor. More particularly, the figure of the father in the act of sacrificing his son is the iconic moment of the metaphor.

In terms of *metaphora*, the question is, from whence does this figure of temptation draw its meaning? The answer is, from the relationship of the father to the son; particularly, from the expression of that relationship in verse 2: 'Take now thy son, thine only son Isaac, whom thou lovest'. The movement of the action is significantly influenced by this metaphoric effect; and the semantic interaction precipitated by the iconic moment of verse 10 is imaginatively grounded in this central relationship whereby action is insistently rooted in Abraham's relationship with his son. So far as this particular text is concerned, the action is not grounded in Abraham's obedience to God, although that is obviously important. It is this obedience which is being tested. But the focus that generates the semantic interaction, and therefore the meaning, is the relationship with his son which is fundamental in grasping the narrative.

In the 'Authorized Version' the rhythmic cadence coming at the end of a sentence, where the conjunction is a mark of the sentence structure, mediates a persuasive effect that the dramatic movement has meaning.[14] The insistent cadence of a downward stress is experienced as an assurance that the narrative will not lead to a sense of fragmentation and chaos. This contrasts, for example, with those poets who have attempted to create a sense of uncertainty and insecurity. Thomas Hardy produces this effect in his poem, *The Voice*. The poem begins in the style of a swinging ballad that gives way to an unhappy listlessness of movement expressive of Hardy's loss and desolation in the breakdown of the verse form in the last stanza.[15] The pattern of cadence in the movement between verse 2 and verse 10 of the Biblical narrative resonates with a seemingly dynamic urgency. By this regular rhythmic, measured fall in relation to the narrative's movement of action, the reader appropriates a sense that the action is moving to a climax, even a sense of resolution or completion. This does not mean that the pattern of cadence ensures that the love of Abraham for his son is carried through the action to become the defining feature in the figure of the sacrificial act, but plays a key element in the reader's grasp of this figure.

The stress pattern of the narrative prose rhythm is, for the most part, directly related to the verb structure. This is combined with a tendency to monosyllabic verbs with an incisive, crisp sound that resonates with a sense of a positive beat in the rhythmic movement. Each action is combined with an anticipatory stress. The stress pattern begins in verse 1 with an almost relaxed pace leading to a flowing, modulated rhythm in verse 2 which mediates a sense of the intimacy and closeness of father and son, and the grave nature of the command. Verse 3 changes the mood to one of commitment and determination with the stress on the practical needs of responding to the command. Then in verse 3 the sound and resonance mediates a holding back with an upward tone of 'lifted up' and 'saw'. The reader feels the hesitancy and disturbance in Abraham's movement towards the climax. Even the cadence of assurance is mingled with this disturbance in an impression of a struggle between a rise and fall in 'afar off'. The holding back is maintained in verse 5, but with the stress upon a different tone in 'abide' and 'worship' mediating a diversion of revival; a kind of 'stopping for breath' in a determination to complete the course. Here the cadence is the clear fall of trust and conviction. The pace picks up again in verse 6 with a similar stress pattern to verse 3, and once more is held up in verse 7 and 8. This time the focus of stress is upon the son. But it is the son in relation to Abraham, and therefore the figure of Abraham remains the centre of attention. The holding back is not one of hesitancy but curiosity and trust, and Abraham's response of paternal assurance. Verse 9 repeats the pattern of verses 3 and 6 so that the movement from verse 2 to verse 10 is maintained throughout the narrative with a dominant practical sense of action as the essential ontological dynamic of the metaphoric semantic interaction precipitated by the iconic moment in verse 10. The stress pattern of the climactic moment in the narrative is one of the three ringing tones of a bell – 'stretched', 'took' and 'slay'. At the moment in the reader's habitation of the narrative's perspective, the ringing resonates with a trembling in the

Kierkegaardian sense.[16] The trembling is the effect of an *ontological sonority* mediated through the productive imagination in the reader's creative response to the figure of Abraham in this moment when his love for his son informs the act of sacrifice. This is not a response of cognitive understanding, but the disclosure of a figure, in the Heideggerian sense,[17] which becomes the focus of the metaphoric iconic moment.

Sound and Imaginative Vision

There is a unity of sound and imaginative vision in this creative process of disclosure. It is analogous to the sculptor's creative activity in disclosing the image in and through the material medium. The sculptor works with the marble or stone. His creativity is tactile, and allied with the particularity of the medium. He chooses his material carefully, sensitive to its touch by which he may discern the possibilities of disclosure. Even then, he must engage in a creative relationship with the chosen object in the revelatory process of his work. So too, the sensitive reader is responsive to the objective materiality of prose rhythm in terms of its sound and the effect of its resonance in relation to an act of configuration, or metaphoric figure. The rhythm is the material medium of the creative, figurative act. It is the dynamic materiality which gives impetus and convergence in the disclosure of the figure. The prose rhythm of the Biblical text is the medium that makes possible the reader's grasp of a figure of a loving father in the act of sacrificing his son by which he or she is given understanding. The figure affirms a sense that this is not an irrational act. It provokes the reader to seek a rational explanation. Prose rhythm is the medium of the productive imagination. It is not the figure that may be disclosed in the work of the imagination but, to draw upon another analogy, the texture and weave of the figure.

The Instant of Affirmation

The act of grasping the metaphoric figure of the iconic moment is analogous to the moment of poetic vision, for example, expressed by Gerard Manley Hopkins in his poem *God's Grandeur* when the sight of a bird in flight, caught by the sun, captures a sense of divine presence in the world:

> Oh, the morning, at the brown brink eastwards, springs –
> Because the Holy Ghost over the bent
> World broods with warm breast and with ah! bright wings.

The reader of 'Abraham's Sacrifice' appropriates the trembling resonance of the iconic moment, inhabiting the Other's ontological perspective upon a figure which mediates profound meaning beyond the seemingly absurd, tragic moment, and affirmation involves an instant of relinquishing self reflection. It is the achievement of an ontological vehemence in the metaphor's power of re-description. Such re-description comes only by means of an instant of abandoning rational description. It is a loss of Self in the Other in the rediscovery of Self in relation to an open horizon of the hermeneutical spiral. It potentially, and actually involves, an intense, penetrating act of perception analogous to T.S. Eliot's attempt to express Thomas Becket's moment of vision in *Murder in the Cathedral*:

> I have had a tremor of bliss, a wink of heaven, a whisper,
> And I would no longer be denied; all things
> Proceed to a joyful consummation.

It is an affirmation of an ontological grounding of Self in the perspective of the Other in the process of a creative grasp of meaning that opens the horizon of reason to continuing interpretation and rational description. But the inherent propensity of reason is definition. The logical structures of cognition are intrinsically unambiguous, and semantically founded upon univocity. Metaphoric ontological vehemence in uprooting the univocity of a literal meaning to interact between semantic fields is therefore a dynamic shattering of cognitive resistance in an instant of affirmation. The ontological trembling is the effect of this shattering and recovery of cognition in a new spatial pattern. This is analogous to shaking the kaleidoscope: the shattering of one pattern in the instant of creating a new one.

In *The Concept of Dread*, Kierkegaard attempts to define this notion of *instant* in his interpretation of Plato's conception in *Parmenides*:

> It is assumed that unity (τὸ ἕν) is and is not, and then it is shown what the consequence will be for it and for the rest. The instant now appears to be that strange being (ἄτοπον – the Greek word is admirably chosen) which lies between movement and repose, without occupying any time; and to this and out of this 'the moving' passes over into the rest, and 'the reposing' into movement. The instant therefore becomes the general category of transition (μεταβολ–); for Plato shows that the instant is related in the same way to the transition from unity to plurality and from plurality to unity, from likeness to unlikeness, etc., it is the instant in which there is neither ἕν nor πολλά, neither discrimination nor integration.
> (*The Concept of Dread*, p. 75)

In the instant of grasping the metaphoric figure, the tension of the *is* and the *is not* in the semantic interaction of the *metaphora* is transcended by the power of the productive imagination generated by the ontological sonority in the dialectic between Self and Other. It is transcended by the power of the imagination reorganizing, within the instant, a unified perception of the world and, consequently, the rational 'space'.

Notes

1. See Chapter 7, 'The Creative Imagination'.
2. See George Steiner's essay, 'A Preface to the Hebrew Bible', *No Passion Spent*, pp. 53–7.
3. See T.R. Henn's *The Bible as Literature*, pp. 38–40. With respect to the significance of cadence in the relationship of prose and poetry, see Seamus Heaney's essay, 'The Makings of Music', in *Preoccupations*: 'The given line, the phrase or cadence which haunts the ear and the eager parts of the mind, this is the tuning fork to which the overall melodies are worked or calculated', (p. 61).
4. See *The History of the English Language*, Chapter 8, 'The Renaissance, 1500–1600', pp. 232–45.
5. Although the themes of obedience to God and the covenantal relationship are inextricably part of Abraham's faith, and therefore his motives for decision and action, the fundamental love of the father for his son, made clear in the narrative, cannot be ignored in terms of its decisive influence upon the particular sacrificial act, and consequently that which is seemingly incomprehensible. This is the essential nature of the singularity of the act, and the secret between God and Abraham to which Kierkegaard and Derrida refer.
6. In this narrative, the metaphorical figure is not in terms of a single word, but a verbal structure which, in the process of reading, gives rise to an 'implicit' metaphor. See Northrop Frye's *The Great Code*, pp. 57–9.
7. The sacrificial act is not a substitution for expiation or propitiation of sins, and a relationship of obedience, *it is* an act of these fundamental characteristics of the ancient cultic ritual of sacrifice. See entry for 'Sacrifice' in *The New Bible Dictionary*.
8. See Kierkegaard's, 'Speech in Praise of Abraham' in *Fear and Trembling*, pp. 49–56.
9. See Derrida's critique of Heideggerian onto-theology and negative theology in his essay, 'Différance', in *Margins of Philosophy*. Also, see a commentary on his relationship with negative theology in John D. Caputo's *The Prayers and Tears of Jacques Derrida*, chapter 1, §1 '*God Is Not* différance'.
10. Derrida's appropriation of Kierkegaard's notions of secrecy and silence conveys the view of the incomprehension of Abraham's act. See *The Gift of Death*, pp. 57–61.
11. See Levinas's *Totality and Infinity*, Section 1A, 1. 'Desire for the Invisible', pp. 33–5.
12. See Levinas's essay, 'Transcendence and Height' in *Basic Philosophical Writings*.
13. See *Time and Narrative*, Vol. 3, pp. 76–7.
14. This rhythmic structure of the narrative is integrally related to the metaphoric configuring effect of the iconic moment of verse 10 so that it is incorporated into the dynamic of the ontological vehemence which precipitates the semantic interaction and the probability of new meaning.
15. The first three verses take the following form:
    Woman much missed, how you call to me, call to me,
    Saying that now you are not as you were
    When you had changed from the one who was all to me,
    But as at first, when our day was fair.

The final verse is:
>   Thus I ; Faltering forward
>   Leaves oozing around me falling,
>   Wind oozing thin through the thorn norward,
>   And the woman calling.

16. See *Fear and Trembling* and the notion of the 'dizziness of freedom' in the *Concept of Dread*, p. 55. See also Derrida's *The Gift of Death*, pp. 53–6.
17. See 'The Origin of the Work of Art' in *Basic Writings*, particularly, p. 189.

Chapter 7

The Creative Imagination

The critical difference between the approach of this study and the rational philosophies of Descartes, Kant and Husserl is the fundamental role of the imagination as the expressive mediation of the ontological foundation for a rational 'space'. In contrast, each of these have attempted to ground the rational structures of the mind directly in an *a priori*, transcendental foundation.

Kant's Notion of the Productive Imagination

The imagination does indeed play a key part in Kant's *Critique of Pure Reason* and the *Critique of Judgment*, and his notion of the productive imagination. Kant's aim is to validate rational unity by means of an ahistorical, transcendental subjective foundation. According to Kant, although the mind is rooted in the world through sensible intuition, it is not dependent upon empirical faculties in its power to think rationally. The original unity of rational thought is direct, and outside of history in terms of the transcendental structures of the mind. In contrast, my aim is to validate the unity of a perspective in which rational reflection is probable, and which is linguistically mediated through texts that are temporally structured, and is, therefore, historically mediated. Consequently, it is a unity that is not free from historical change. Fundamentally, the source of this unity is the dialectical relationship between the Self and Other. The unity of a rational perspective is grounded in a relationship of the Self with the Other in terms of a reader's appropriation and habitation of the narrative identity of a text.

Kant defines the role played by the imagination in his First and Third Critiques. In the Preface to the Second Edition of the *Critique of Pure Reason*, Kant writes,

> it should be possible to have knowledge of objects *a priori*, determining something in regard to them prior to their being given ...
> (*Critique of Pure Reason*, tr. Norman Kemp Smith, p. 22)

He claims that knowledge of objects, although determined by sensibility, is founded upon *a priori* principles of intuition that he endows with a formal character which he calls the 'science of all principles' and terms the 'Transcendental Aesthetic'.[1] According to Kant, the appearance of sense phenomena in consciousness is represented in cognition under the synthetic control of the *a priori* principles of intuition by means of the faculty of the imagination. This synthesis, which he calls, the 'Transcendental Synthesis', is the effect of the imaginative power to schematize a conceptual manifold which brings together, which 'grasps', the empirical phenomena represented in empirical form. It is a judgment of understanding with respect to the appearance of objects in a rational form.

There are, however, two modes of the role of the imagination in the *Critique of Pure Reason*. The productive mode relates the cognitive process to the *a priori* principles, or categories of reason, while the *reproductive* mode ensures that the schematization of the conceptual manifold is based upon sense experience. In reference to these two modes, he writes,

> I sometimes also entitle it the *productive* imagination, to distinguish it from the *reproductive* imagination, whose synthesis is entirely subject to empirical laws, namely, of association, and which therefore contributes nothing to the explanation of the possibility of *a priori*   knowledge. The reproductive synthesis falls within the domain, not of transcendental philosophy, but of psychology.
> (*Ibid.*, #24 B152, p. 165)

Kant entitles the reproductive synthesis of the manifold of sensible intuition, the *figurative* synthesis.[2] This gives form to the representation of the appearance of sense experience in consciousness; and this reproduction of the form of appearance by the figurative synthesis of the empirical imagination is made possible by the Transcendental Aesthetic of pure intuition and form. He writes,

> That in which alone the sensations can be posited and ordered in a certain form, cannot itself be sensation; and, therefore, while the matter of appearance is given to us *a posteriori* only, its form must lie already for sensations *a priori* in the mind, and so must allow of being considered apart from all sensations.
> (*Ibid.*, # B34 p. 66)

The Transcendental Aesthetic not only determines extension and figure, but the intuitive sense of time and space.[3] This is the mode of the productive imagination, which Kant develops as a creative faculty in the *Critique of Judgment*.

Kant's aim in the first part of the Third Critique is to show how the subjective capacity of the human mind establishes notions of taste, beauty and the sublime. The productive mode becomes the means of defining the imagination as a creative faculty in the mind of the genius.[4] whereas the reproductive mode continually brings back to the mind an exhibition of the forms which have been received through empirical intuition. The productive mode has the power of original exhibition; it is a creative power that gives birth to *aesthetic ideas* which are the counterpart of *rational ideas*. By the former, Kant does not mean determinate concepts but refers to a mode of presentation which sets intellectual thought in motion.[5]

The productive mode of the imagination is a faculty with the capacity to create an original presentation of images in terms of the free play of the imagination acting upon cognition to expand conceptual meaning. By means of the creative capacity of the imagination, the rational subject may increase understanding of his or her experience of the objective world. But this understanding is determined by a rational unity founded upon the transcendental subject and not upon the objective world. Although sensible intuition is the basis for the creative capacity of the imagination, unity is derived from the *a priori* categorical structures of the mind, and *transcendental apperception* as the foundation of the thinking subject. It is these critical aspects of unity which need careful consideration.

Kant's understanding of the unity of the categories of rational thought was, in the early writings, taken over from the traditional transcendental sense of unity derived from the unity of the supreme being. Although in the *Critique of Pure Reason* he seeks to reduce this to a category of quantity, he is also concerned to emphasize the extra-categorical sense of unity as the basis of all logical functions in the judgment of rational thought. The significance of this lies in his attempt to develop a system of transcendental philosophy as the foundation for science to resolve the 'endless controversies' on the 'battleground' of metaphysics. He writes,

> Had the ancients ever conceived such a notion (i.e. the *a priori* unity of judging and the pure concepts of the understanding), doubtless the whole study of the pure rational knowledge, which under the name of metaphysics has for centuries spoiled many a sound mind, would have reached us in quite another shape, and would have enlightened the human understanding, instead of actually exhausting it in obscure and vain speculation, thereby rendering it unfit for true science.
> (*Prolegomena to Any Future Metaphysics*, p. 87)

Kant's notion of transcendental unity is unconditioned and is the foundation of synthetic unity which is thought in the categories. Apperception plays the central role in this foundation of transcendental unity. That is, apperception as the source of original unity which is the foundation of the thinking subject; in other words, transcendental apperception that lies beyond thought and is the unchanging unity of the subject's identity, in contrast to what Kant terms *empirical apperception*. He writes,

> This original and transcendental condition is no other than *transcendental apperception*. Consciousness of self according to the determinations of our state in inner perception is merely empirical, and always changing. No fixed and abiding self can present itself in this flux of inner appearances. Such consciousness is usually named *inner sense*, or *empirical apperception*. What has *necessarily* to be represented numerically identical cannot be thought as such through empirical data. To render such a transcendental presupposition valid, there must be a condition which precedes all experience, and which makes experience itself possible ...

The numerical unity of this apperception is thus the *a priori* ground of all concepts ...
(*Critique of Pure Reason*, A107, p. 136)

The productive mode of the imagination is, therefore, on the one hand, based upon sensible intuition, but, on the other, determined by the original unity of transcendental apperception in terms of the achievement of greater understanding. This mode of the imagination is dependent upon sense experience of objects in creating *aesthetic ideas*, or the exhibition of new forms, by promoting and regulating a cognitive response in conceptual development and expansion. It is the dynamic capacity aesthetically to restructure sensible intuition in a creative power of presentation promoting thought. For example, the imaginative perception of a tree, based upon the sensible intuition of the object as a tree, may create an aesthetic idea of the majesty, or dignity or nobility of the tree which promotes rational thought in the conceptual descriptions and explanations of this idea.[6] But the foundation of the latter is the original unity of subjective identity. In contrast to the creativity of the imagination, this unity is not dynamic. It is unchanging and ahistorical, otherwise, according to Kant, there is no possibility of validating conceptual unity as the basis for rational thought.

The Productive Imagination and Ontological Perspective

Kant claims that the unity of consciousness, transcendental apperception, makes possible the purest objective unity in the *a priori* concepts of time and space, and is thus the *a priori* ground of all concepts. It is that 'mysterious power' which 'makes judging possible'. The problem with Kant's transcendental philosophy is the issue of temporality. Transcendental apperception is outside of temporality. If consciousness is always and essentially historical, that is, if the conscious 'I', self-consciousness, not only inherently possesses a past, present and future but is conditioned by being-in-the-world in terms of the Heideggerian notion of *Dasein*, then the unity of consciousness cannot lie beyond history. The source of this unity must lie within history.

My aim is to show that this unity, defined in terms of the identity of self-consciousness, is grounded in the ontological perspective of a linguistically structured lifeworld. This perspective is not limited to a particular way of seeing the world, it is a perspective of habitation; it is a way of inhabiting a lifeworld. To inhabit a lifeworld is to appropriate an inherent way of being-in-the-world, an ontological perspective, a unity of being, and consequently a unity of identity, a unity of self-consciousness.

My aim is not to validate conceptual unity *per se*, but to establish the perspective of a lifeworld that makes sense, and is, therefore, a unified view which may be rationally described and interpreted.[7] The productive mode of the imagination is the means of appropriating this perspective in terms of an iconic moment of metaphor, and an act of configuration, of grasping a text. This is comparable to the Kantian notion of the creative capacity of the imagination, but instead of structuring sensible intuition in terms of an aesthetic idea, it posits a creative capacity, in terms of figuration, of an ontological act of appropriation and habitation. In contrast to reflection being provoked by an aesthetic idea, it is through the imaginative habitation of a lifeworld. The productive imagination is ontologically grounded and is the dynamic mediation of the unity of an ontological perspective. In relation to the mediation of temporal narratives, this is the power which roots rational thought in history with an horizon open to endless interpretation.

Linguistic mediation is a key difference between these contrasting views of the imagination.[8] The productive mode of the imagination has the capacity to grasp linguistic figuration in a creative response to unify a pattern of mediated particular, concrete, sensual images.[9] It is the nature of this mediation that marks the critical difference from the Kantian understanding. Ricoeurean theories make clear the importance of the symbolic characteristics of metaphor and narrative, and their significance in terms of mediation. By means of these symbolic characteristics, the reader participates in, appropriates and inhabits a linguistically mediated active state of affairs which involves a drive to make sense of this activity.

The grounding of the conscious and cognitive features of this drive is corporeal and ontological. It is on the 'edge' of and lies beyond consciousness in the way that Merleau-Ponty defines *operative* intentionality. Therefore, the grasping of the text by the productive mode of the imagination not only 'makes reason think more' in the manner of the Kantian notion, but also grounds rational thought in a dynamic, teleological drive whereby unity is achieved by means of a dialectic between 'suspicion' and 'affirmation'.[10]

Foundation of Rational Unity

The productive imagination is a way of being in the world of the Other; the means of appropriating the ontological perspective of narrative identity. This is not an act of passive observation, but an ontological vehemence in the drive towards total involvement which is a thorough disturbance of consciousness.[11] Consequently, it is a disturbance of operative intentionality as the dynamic convergence towards unity. The nature of this disturbance is the active state of affairs mediated through prose rhythm, and the expressive effect in terms of bodily resonance. The faculty of the imagination is creative in relation to the resonance of corporeal rhythm, and the disturbance of operative intentionality.[12] As a result, there is a centripetal effect with regard to conscious particular intentionality which is the basis of an ontological perspective, or, in Kantian terms, a schematism of the conceptual manifold.

The provocation of rational thought by the productive imagination's grasp of the narrative is grounded in an ontological vehemence in the drive towards unity. Imaginatively, the reader is provoked to understand the world of the text in terms of inhabiting that world. It is the world of the Other that challenges rational thought to be open to its horizon of meaning by relinquishing any absolute sense of unity in order to affirm a new sense of unity; a new meaning, that is, in order to understand and make sense of the world of the Other. But the Self, which is provoked into reflection by imaginative habitation, relinquishes conceptual unity, upon which its identity depends, within a Kierkegaardian *instant*. Within that instant, it is the ontological vehemence which is sustained in terms of Sonorous Being as the moment of affirmation.[13] In this sense, the source of affirmation is beyond consciousness but determines the conscious intentional drive towards unity in terms of the relationship between operative and particular intentionalities.

But if the moment of affirmation is beyond consciousness, how is such affirmation possible? If affirmation of a unity of being in terms of an ontological perspective upon a lifeworld is achieved beyond consciousness, and is not an affirmation of conceptual unity free from suspicion, what is the nature of that affirmation and its relationship with conceptual unity? How is such affirmation possible if rational thought is never free from suspicion?

Corporeal Intentionality and Sonorous Concordance

In the example of 'Abraham's sacrifice' my aim was to show how it may be possible to gain an understanding of this story without complete explanation; that is, to imaginatively inhabit the lifeworld of the narrative by means of the prose rhythm of the 'Authorized Version' so that the reader becomes totally absorbed and loses himself, or herself, in the text. In such an act of reading there may be a moment, an instant, when self-identity becomes one with the narrative identity. This can only happen if there is the possibility of grasping a viewpoint, a perspective, whereby intentionality, the drive to understand, is grounded in corporeally expressed ontological concordance.[14] As the reader attempts to inhabit the world of this seemingly absurd and tragic act, there is discordance in his state of being, and an active disturbance expressed in his body and consciousness. But the prose rhythm that mediates the ontological condition of the world of the narrative, and is corporeally appropriated by the reader, resonates with a sense of concordance as the reader reflects upon the story – a concordance which affects operative intentionality at the 'edge' of and beyond consciousness. It is this concordance which is the ontological grounding of an affirmation of the perspectival unity . It is the fundamental appropriation of the activity of the story, particularly the central act of Abraham's sacrifice, through the mediation of the prose rhythm that makes possible a sense of concordance, and therefore an affirmation of an ontological perspective. The imaginative active habitation of the story by the mediation of prose rhythm resonates with a concordance affirming a conviction that the story does make sense, and the drive to reflect, interpret and explain is continually sustained.

The discordance of conscious disturbance caused by reading the story of 'Abraham's sacrifice' is the extreme provocation of the questions, 'What does this mean?' and 'How can it be explained?' Any affirmation of a rational resolution of these questions must involve reflection; and if any attempted resolution by reflective analysis and interpretation is suspect then affirmation is suspect. The problem here seems to lie in the apparent attribution of rational affirmation to the sonorous characteristics of an ontological perspective. What is the relationship between this sonority and reflection? This question is more problematic if it is conceded that rational unity is never free from suspicion.

Operative intentionality is the centripetal dynamic, at the 'edge' and beyond consciousness, which drives conscious particular intentionality focused upon the image of a concrete, particular act. In the example of Abraham's act of raising the knife to sacrifice his son, the imaginative power to grasp that act as the focus of configuration to give a sense of meaning to the story is the ontological sonorous concordance expressed in the dynamic of operative intentionality. As the reader appropriates and inhabits the story, there is a movement of resonance, mediated by prose rhythm, from discordance to concordance whereby the image is grasped by means of the dynamic of operative and particular intentionalities. In other words, operative and particular intentionalities are fundamental characteristics of the creative power of the imagination.[15]

The grasping of the focal image is a configuring act grounded upon the movement from discordance to concordance. In the process of this act, the effect of concordance is the imaginative achievement to perceive an image that draws together, that is, configures, the whole narrative in a unity which provokes and promotes rational explanation. It is to grasp the image of Abraham in the act of sacrificing his son in such a way that every particular concrete aspect of his relationship with his son are united in an image which vehemently uproots the semantic discord in reflection to configure the narrative in the drive to achieve a resolution, or semantic concordance, in understanding.[16]

Distanciation and the Primordial Dialectic

In such a way the imagination creates a perspective upon the lifeworld of the Other which is dialectically related to rational reflection. It is the appropriation of the prose rhythm of the Abraham story that configures the narrative which makes rational explanation of an initially seeming absurdity potentially available.[17] Equally, the reader's reflection upon the sacrificial act plays an integral role in achieving the unity of an ontological perspective. In this sense, suspicion does not have a negative effect, but is critical in the drive towards affirmation.

Reflection takes place within the world created by the imagination. Ricoeur calls this *distanciation*.[18] In contrast to the Kantian transcendental rational structures of the mind that are not subject to historical change, distanciation is always within history, and the imaginative creative act which, as it were, sets the scene for habitation and reflection. As the reader inhabits the lifeworld configured by the imagination focused upon the image of the act of sacrifice, he or she is driven to reflect in relation to the imaginative grasping of the unity of the image. This unity, achieved by the dynamic of particular intentionality, gives impetus to the reflective process in terms of the drive to understand in continuing interpretation and explanation. It is the primordial dialectic of distanciation between understanding founded upon the power of the imagination, and explanation of rational thought. Within this dialectic, 'affirmation' is achieved as a perspectival unity upon the imaginatively inhabited lifeworld which promotes rational reflection, while 'suspicion' relates to conceptual unity in terms of the word as the basic unit of rational thought and explanation. The foundation for 'affirmation' is mediated through the figurative, or 'poetic' mode of the total narrative with the sentence as the basic unit, whereas conceptual unity, in terms of the word as the basic unit, is never free from 'suspicion' because continuing interpretation is the basis of rational explanation.[19]

In the story of 'Abraham's sacrifice' it is the prose rhythm of the 'Authorized Version' which gives momentum to this movement towards the act of Abraham raising the knife to make the fatal strike. It is in the pattern of sound of the prose rhythm that the reader imaginatively perceives the various images of activity grasped in a configuration focused upon the act on Mount Moriah, at the same time as reflecting upon these actions. The images of the loving father taking his son on a fateful journey; the actions of the trusting son oblivious of his father's intentions; the apparent hesitancy along the way; the preparations for the sacrifice; and the climactic moment: all are drawn together in the reader's imagination by the sense of concordance in the effect of the prose rhythm. The reader is driven by the effect of the prose rhythm to affirm that this world does make sense; that this act of a loving father sacrificing his own son is not absurd. Therefore his attempt to rationally explain this act, although unresolved in any absolute sense, and, consequently, not free from 'suspicion', may be held within a dialectic of 'affirmation' and 'suspicion'. In other words, an explanation may be provisionally affirmed in terms of potential availability in the process of continuing interpretation.

Metaphor and the Creation of Meaning

Understanding is affirmed not by the focal image of an act of configuration alone, but by a metaphonic iconic moment which vehemently uproots a literal meaning into a process of semantic interaction whereby a new meaning is created. The significance of the interactive theory of metaphor is that a new meaning is created which potentially, and in time actually, expands and develops conceptual thought. It is not simply the creation of an ontological perspective but a conceptual enlargement in response to an open horizon. In the story of 'Abraham's sacrifice', verses 1 to 10 should be read as a metaphor. The reader's attention focuses upon the metaphoric image of the sacrificial act in verse 10 in grasping the meaning of the narrative and a greater understanding than is gained through the literal, conceptual meaning of the words. A new meaning of this sacrificial act is opened up by the imaginative, figurative appropriation of the metaphor. The literal meaning of the sentence, 'And Abraham stretched forth his hand, and took the knife to slay his son', is uprooted by the metaphoric image which mediates a vehement interaction between this meaning and the whole narrative, particularly the words, 'Take thou thy son, thine only son Isaac, whom thou lovest'. As the reader endeavours to understand the story, to grasp the viewpoint of the narrative, the power of the imagination transcends any conceptual inhibitions by a figurative dynamic that uproots and suspends the literal meaning in an imaginative response to an open semantic horizon. The literal meaning of a father in the act of killing his son is suspended in the reader's ontological grasp of the configuration of the narrative focused upon the metaphoric image. The reader responds to the possibility of a new meaning while imaginatively inhabiting the activity of the story. There is a discordance in his or her state of being initially provoked by an attempt to reflect upon the meaning of the act. But the reader's imaginative response to the metaphoric image in an iconic moment overcomes the cognitive resistance of this discordance whereby this agitation of his or her state of being is resonantly directed towards a concordance and semantic innovation. The prose rhythm of the text is the mediation of the active condition of inhabiting the story. To understand the story is not fundamentally imaginatively to perceive, or to reflect, but corporeally to inhabit the activity of the narrative. It is the reader's active condition in terms of his or her sonorous state of being which imaginatively animates the figuration giving rise to semantic interaction and innovation. Although consciously the reader may be unaware of the effect of prose rhythm, her imagination is dynamically grounded in this effect in her sonorous state of being. It is this dynamic appropriation and habitation, grounded in an ontological vehemence, which uproots the literal reference of the sacrificial act to achieve, by semantic interaction, what Ricoeur calls, a second order, metaphorical reference;[20] that is, an imaginative, ontologically generated reference which is directed through and beyond the linguistic semantic inhibitions of literal, conceptual meaning to an active image which opens up a new meaning.

This view of the imagination and metaphor is a key issue in contemporary philosophical debate, particularly with respect to those who claim that not only is there no foundation for 'truth', but that denotation is irrelevant and misleading. It is the creative capacity of the imagination in terms of the poetic mode of language to change the perspective, to inaugurate new ways of thinking in relation to experience. For example, in his report on the state of knowledge in the Western world, Jean-François Lyotard writes,

> Given equal competence (no longer in the acquisition of knowledge, but in its production), what extra performity depends on in the final analysis is 'imagination,' which allows one either to make a new move or change the rules of the game. (*Postmodern Condition*, p. 52)

Metaphor plays a central role in this philosophical concern for the creative capacity of the imagination in the continual change of perspective upon historical experience. The work of Friedrich Nietzsche is an important influence upon the philosophical perspectival view, and what he terms, 'the primitive world of metaphor' in this primordial activity of the 'artistically creating subject'. For Nietzsche, language is informed by the primal energy of the artistic subject whose creative power is revealed in world production as an infinite regress of images. According to Nietzsche, language is essentially an amoeba-like sensuous figurative mode of continuously changing metaphors which are forgotten in relation to the cognitive, conceptual mode as the process of use wears away the consciousness of figuration, as the images of coins are worn away. Derrida makes use of this metaphor of the coin which Ricoeur criticizes in their early exchange of views in Derrida's 'White Mythology' in *Margins of Philosophy*, Ricoeur's Study 8 in *The Rule of Metaphor*, and Derrida's response in *The Retrait of Metaphor*. A fundamental difference lies in interactive theory of metaphor which makes a clear division between the figurative and semantic characteristics of metaphor.

It is this understanding of metaphor which is distinct from those who commend relinquishing any notion of 'truth', or affirmation of rational unity, in favour of unleashing the imaginative power of world-production.[21] Although this critical difference provides a way of understanding a hermeneutical process in which rational unity may be affirmed, the fundamental issue provoked by Nietzsche, and contemporary philosophers such as Lyotard, has not fully addressed the issue of verification.

Notes

1. See Kant's *Critique of Pure Reason*, A77–9, B103–5.
2. *Ibid.*, B151.
3. *Ibid.*, A37–9, B54–6.
4. See *Critique of Judgment*, Part 1 § 49, 314–15.
5. *Ibid.*, 315.
6. See note 4. Also *Critique if Judgment*, § 57, Comment I.
7. In his conclusion to *The Rule of Metaphor*, Ricoeur states, 'What is given to thought in this way by the "tensional" truth of poetry is the most primordial, most hidden dialectic – the dialectic that reigns between the experience of belonging

as a whole and the power of distanciation that opens up the space of speculative thought' (p. 313). See also his essay, 'The Hermeneutical function of distanciation', in *Hermeneutics and the Human Sciences*, Part II, 4.

8. Ricoeur is concerned to make clear that the constitution of presentation (*Darstellung*), preceded and supports the linguistic medium which it summons, and that the reference of language back to the structure of experience is the most important presupposition of hermeneutics. See *Hermeneutics and the Human Sciences*, pp. 117–18. However, the view in this study is that Ricoeur's understanding of the relationship between language and presentation must be complemented by Merleau-Ponty's linguistic phenomenology, for example, when he states, 'Language is much more like a sort of being than a means, and that is why it can present something to us so well.' *Signs*, p. 43.

9. See *Time and Narrative*, Vol. 1 p. 68.

10. The problematic of the notion of unity is identified in the early writings of Ricoeur in, for example, *History and Truth* in the chapter on 'Negativity and Primary Affirmation'; and in Book III, chapter 3, 'Dialectic: Archaeology and Teleology' in *Freud and Philosophy*. This theme is central to the development of his hermeneutical philosophy appearing in his later writing, *Oneself as Another*, with respect to the dialectic between Self and Other and the issue of the unity of self-attestation. This study attempts to develop the analysis of the dialectic between 'suspicion' and 'affirmation' in terms of discordance and concordance of Sonorous Being.

11. It disturbs the viewpoint of consciousness affecting every aspect of perception in a discordance between the present's inherited perspective and the ontological dynamic of a refocusing of this perspective. This may be compared with Gadamer's fusion of horizons in the hermeneutical process. See *Truth and Method*, pp. 302–7.

12. This is analogous to the process of adjustment in inhabiting an alien culture. It is an intentional, active, corporeal process. The rhythmic patterns of cultural activity effect a physical process which is the grounding of the conscious intention to achieve an appropriate condition of living in a new world.

13. In the mode of reflection, affirmation cannot escape suspicion but it is sustained by a teleological conviction grounded in the instant at the ontological and corporeal levels which lies at the 'edge' and beyond consciousness.

14. In *Time and Narrative*, vol. 1, Ricoeur attempts to define the plot with respect to the notion of Emplotment as 'A Model of Concordance' (see pp. 38–42). In his reading of Aristotle's *Poetics*, he identifies Melody as the feature of *mimesis* as that which interests him with respect to the importance of linguistic rhythm in the imitation or representation of action (p. 33). Furthermore, he notes the play of discordance internal to concordance in Aristotle's theory of tragic plots (p. 38). He does not however appear to develop the significance of the role of rhythm as an ontological grounding of affirmation.

15. Imagination is here defined not simply in terms of a faculty but the dynamic of a condition of being-in-the-world.

16. The dynamic process of configuration, effected by the iconic moment of the sacrificial act in verse 10, uproots the literal reference of this act in terms of the act of a father killing his son to create a second-order metaphorical reference by means of an interaction within the semantic structures of the narrative with particular emphasis upon the relationship between verse 2 and verse 10. This

second-order reference is a teleological drive towards the unity of the love of the father and the sacrificial act.

17. Throughout the analysis of this study there is an attempt to move towards the notion of 'probability' with respect to Affirmation. At this stage, the analysis has not reached the point where this notion may be used since the important criterion of attestation has not been considered. For this reason, the notion of 'potentially available' is being used. The significance of the notion of 'probability' is included in chapter 8 and corresponding notes.

18. See 'The Hermeneutical Function of Distanciation' in Ricoeur's *From Text to Action*, chapter 3. For a useful commentary, see Leonard Lawlor's *Imagination and Chance*, Part II, 'Ricoeur's Notion of Distanciation'.

19. In the relation of the word and sentence in the process of continuing interpretation, Ricoeur's theory of metaphor is fundamental. See his essay, 'Metaphor and the Main Problem of Hermeneutics in *A Ricoeur Reader: Reflection and the Imagination*, ed. Mario J. Valdés.

20. See Study 7, 'Metaphor and Reference' in *The Rule of Metaphor.*

21. The notion of linguistic world production is an important theme in contemporary debate in the philosophy of language. Among its advocates are Jean-François Lyotard (see *The Postmodern Condition*), Richard Rorty (see *Contingency, Irony and Solidarity*), and Nelson Goodman (see *Languages of Art* and *Ways of Worldmaking*).

Chapter 8

Reasonable Hope

The issue of verification in the tradition of logico-empirical philosophy is based upon the principle of verification. In contrast, my aim is to show that there is reasonable hope of affirming rational unity. This is not certainty, but a sustained teleological conviction subjected to a continuing critique in relation to an open hermeneutical horizon. It is the achievement of the dynamic of a primordial dialectic between conviction and critique, understanding and explanation, Self and Other. The latter dyad refers to the nature of the grounding of this dialectic in the reader's imaginatively active habitation of the world of the text, the world of the 'other' in terms of narrative identity. In other words, reasonable hope arises from the affirmation of selfhood in the appropriation of narrative identity.

This raises the critical issue of identity that Ricoeur addresses in *Oneself as Another* in developing the work on narrative identity which he had begun in Volume 3 of *Time and Narrative*. In attempting to grasp the heart of the problem of personal identity, he distinguishes a structural difference between what he terms *idem* identity, or sameness, and *ipse* identity, or selfhood. The former relates to the permanence of identity, particularly with respect to character; whereas the paradigm for the latter is, making a promise. Ricoeur's concern in making this distinction arises from his response to the question 'who?' in relation to 'I can': I can speak, I can act, I can recount, etc. This is the historical 'I' which evades the discursive descriptions of *idem* identity. Narrative identity is the notion that relates the 'who?' of personal identity to temporality which is thematized by narrative.

This examination of personal identity is the central theme of the first six studies of *Oneself as Another* in which Ricoeur investigates the literature of Anglo-Saxon philosophy in this area. In critically acknowledging the importance of defining personal identity in terms of sameness in this rich field of analytical philosophy, it is in relation to otherness, particularly in terms of narrative identity, that an ontological foundation is established. It is in the dialectic between *ipse* identity of making a promise that is willed, sustained and proclaims itself despite of change, and the *idem* identity of sameness that the heart of personal identity resides. But how may the 'I' of personal identity be affirmed? How is affirmation of the historical 'I', whose identity is grounded in the otherness of narrative identity, possible?

But the question that Ricoeur does not fully address is how is affirmation of personal identity possible if it does not escape, or transcend not only sameness but temporality since these are the modes of suspicion? These are the modes in which the capable 'I', to use Ricoeur's language, is inescapably confronted by the question of 'who?' with respect to 'I can ...', and 'I promise'. Must not personal identity transcend the primordial dialectic which lies at its heart if it is to be affirmed? But if it does, how is affirmation possible? This takes the question, moving the debate, to the levels of conviction, or spirituality where identity is renounced, and therefore is a metaphysical issue. Ricoeur does touch upon this question in response to the work of Derek Parfit,[1] and particularly his statement, 'Identity is not what matters'. In Parfit's attack on what he calls the 'self-interest theory',[2] in which a person aims at the outcome of ethical decisions that would best serve himself, he argues for altruism in terms of a renouncement of personal identity. Acknowledging the importance of Parfit's view, Ricoeur claims he has gone too far. He writes,

> I still do not see how the question 'who?' can disappear in the extreme cases in which it remains without an answer. For really, how can we ask ourselves about *what* matters if we could not ask *to whom* the thing mattered or not?
> (*Oneself as Another*, p. 137)

His response is given a clearer focus, particularly in relation to this study, when he further attempts to address a 'crisis *within* selfhood' provoked by Parfit's moral reflection. That is the crisis of different kinds of ownership in terms of 'what I have' and 'who I am', and Parfit's concern in attacking the 'self-interest theory'. Ricoeur writes,

> But is not a moment of self-dispossession essential to authentic selfhood? And must one not, in order to make oneself open, available, belong to oneself in a certain sense? We have already asked: would the question of what matters arise if there were no one to whom the question of identity mattered? Let us now add: if my identity were to lose all importance in every respect, would not the question of others also cease to matter?
> (*Ibid.*, p. 138–9)

In the discussion recorded in *Critique and Conviction* regarding the question of selfhood, he makes a revealing and significant statement,

> I have to fight to the end, then, as a philosopher on behalf of identity, prepared to renounce it – in the strict sense of the word – at another level; we shall return to this no doubt when we talk about religion.
> (*Critique and Conviction*, p. 90)

The critical question is, can selfhood in terms of personal identity be affirmed unless identity is renounced, or preferably, relinquished in an instant of transcendence? What is the nature of affirmation, or is affirmation possible if it is limited to the primordial dialectic? Must not the dialectic between suspicion and affirmation of personal identity be sustained by a transcendental source of affirmation in the loss of this identity? But then, what is the nature of the relationship between this loss and affirmation? Do not the rhythms of the soul, to use the language of religious discourse, play a fundamental role in the 'finding' of the self?

Second-order Reference

Here, I must return to the notion of second-order metaphysical reference in an attempt to determine the nature of this relationship between Sonorous Being and attestation, touched upon in Chapter 2 (pp. 36–7). Attestation of selfhood, among other things, raises the issue of the nature of this second-order reference. If attestation of selfhood is in terms of its mediation through the otherness of narrative identity, what is the nature of the reference with respect to the textual mediation of this identity? More particularly, what is the nature of the second-order reference taking into account the critical questions raised above regarding the loss and affirmation of personal identity?

Affirmation, or attestation also raises semantic questions: what kind of meaning is opened up by this imaginative response to the text? How can this metaphorical reference provide the foundation for universality of conceptual unity? Is it not a purely relative, incommensurable reference? If prose rhythm is its ontological grounding, does this not reveal a certain arbitrary nature? What ensures that prose rhythm may indeed be the dynamic of an extralinguistic reference to an objective, active state of affairs, the being-in-the-world of narrative identity, and not simply the textual means of arousing the imagination in an arbitrary fashion?

What is at issue here is, first, an ontological and phenomenological reference in contrast to the referential relation of word to object of rational description. It is ontological reference in terms of the expression of selfhood compared to an understanding of reference in terms of the Cartesian *cogito*.[3] It is the reference of Self to Other. Secondly, it is a temporal reference; a diachronic, semantic reference, not the ahistorical, synchronic, semiotic reference of structural analysis. It is the reference of discourse as distinct from language. In Saussurean terms, the reference of *parole* rather than *langue*. Thirdly, the basic unit of the former is the sentence which always has an external reference. It is always about something; it refers beyond language to the lifeworld as structured through the imagination. Fourthly, it relates to the experience the reader brings to the world of the text. The referential power of the imagination is, therefore, not only the capacity to refer to something beyond language, but the refiguring of the mediation of the horizon of the Other in relation to experience.

Fifthly, it is a reference of activity. It is a reference to the temporal state of being which is a state of activity. It has the power to create the sensible image in the form of the iconic moment of metaphor and the configuration or emplotment of narrative which is the grasping of an active state of being. In *The Rule of Metaphor*, Ricoeur analyses the difference between Aristotle's *Rhetoric* and *Poetics*, and in particular the expression 'imitation of nature' in terms of *mimesis* and *phusis*:

> Might there not be an underlying relationship between 'signifying active reality' and speaking out *phusis?*
>
> But *mimesis* does not signify only that all discourse is of the world; it does not embody just the referential function of poetic discourse. Being *mimesis phuseos*, it connects this referential function to the revelation of the Real as Act. This is the concept of *phusis* in the expression *mimesis phuseos*, to serve as an *index* for that dimension of reality that does not receive due account in the simple description of that-thing-over-there. To present men '*as acting*' and all things '*as in act*' – such could well be the ontological function of metaphorical discourse, in which every dormant potentiality of existence appears as blossoming forth, every latent capacity for action as actualized.
>
> (*The Rule of Metaphor*, p. 43)

In other words, in grasping reality through the mediation of the text, the transcendent referential power of the imagination creates new meaning and redescribes the textual horizon by enlivening the potentiality of being; that is, by imaginatively setting the possibility of concrete acting beings before the eyes to imaginatively apprehend, through the potential of activity, the temporal perspective of the Other at and beyond the horizon of the text.

Sixthly, the ontological reference is to the actual and potential activity of being, and, therefore, it is to the One who acts. For this reason it is an intersubjective reference. It is a reference between the reader, the Self who imaginatively appropriates the activity mediated by the text, and the 'who' of the text; the 'who' whose presence is mediated through the implicit as well as explicit pronouns, and temporal adverbs. It is the 'who?' of the text which is fundamental in the hermeneutical process rather than the 'what?' in terms of description and analysis. The latter question leaves unresolved the prior question 'who?' which relates not to cause and effect but to motives and intentions. It is this question that gives expression to an encounter with the Other through the appropriation of narrative identity by the Self. This involves a return to the Same,[4] following what Ricoeur calls a detour through the mediation of the linguistic figurative structures,[5] in asking the question 'what?' in the process of understanding and reflection in the hermeneutical spiral.

Attestation: Fantasy or Reality

This second-order reference is not aimed at verification in the sense of determining 'truth' in conceptual terms. Nor is its purpose to establish certainty in the Cartesian tradition.[6] Its aim is what Ricoeur calls *attestation*. In the introduction to *Oneself as Another* he writes,

> Attestation presents itself first, in fact, as a kind of belief. But it is not a doxic belief, in the sense in which *doxa* (belief) has less standing than *episteme* (science, or better, knowledge). Whereas doxic belief is implied in the grammar of 'I believe that', attestation belongs to the grammar of 'I believe in.' It thus links up with testimony, as the etymology reminds us, inasmuch as it is in speech of one giving testimony that one believes. One can call upon no epistemic instance greater than that of belief – or, if one prefers, the credence – that belongs to the triple dialectic of reflection and analysis, of selfhood and sameness, and of self and other.
> (*Oneself as Another*, p. 21)

Although attestation cannot claim any guarantee or foundation in the Cartesian strong sense of attempting to establish it on self-founding theoretical knowledge, and is vulnerable to the permanent threat of suspicion, Ricoeur argues that there is no recourse against suspicion, or false testimony, but a more reliable attestation.[7] However, because of the detour by way of analysis within the hermeneutical process, verification is included as a necessary epistemic moment in reflection.[8] But it is attestation, in the sense of a 'reliable attestation', that validates affirmation because fundamentally it is an attestation of self. It is the essential credence or trust in the power of recognition of oneself as a character in the narrative.

This instant of recognition is analogous to the instant when someone first takes her feet off the bottom of the pool and becomes a swimmer. Her state of being has changed in an instant, and her self-identity is transformed: she is a swimmer. It is a profound act of conversion. It is to see the world and self in a radically new way. It is this conversion which lies at the heart of the problem of the relationship between affirmation and suspicion. What is the basis of trust and conviction in the self's appropriation of a transformed identity? Is such an appropriation made as a result of the suspension or relinquishment of rational reflection? For example, take the case of a child's freeplay of the imagination in appropriating the identity of a fantasy character. It is a way the child learns to develop and enjoy the richness of the imaginative power in creating settings for emotional and psychological experiences in a secure environment protected from the consequences of such play if allowed to roam free in the world outside. Also, the child is aware, or is made to be aware, of the difference between the fantasy world of play and the realities of daily life. It is, however, when the awareness of difference is lost in adulthood that the disturbing problem lies.

In 1605, Miguel de Cervantes published the first part of *Don Quixote* which was to become a classic in European literature. As the conclusion to part II, published in 1615, he writes

> For my sole object has been to arouse men's contempt for all fabulous and absurd stories of knight errantry, whose credit this tale of my genuine Don Quixote has

already shaken, and which will, without a doubt, soon tumble to the ground.
Farewell.
(*Don Quixote*, p. 940)

During the sixteenth century there had been an extraordinary compulsion to
read stories of chivalric romance. Although the vogue for reading these
romances had been in fast decline since the 1580s, it is evident from the above
that Cervantes was still convinced that they needed to be treated as a menace
to good taste. Whether that was true or not, they had been condemned by
many priests and humanist critics for controlling the mind and imagination in
popular culture causing people to live in the fantasy world of romance instead
of the reality of everyday life. The figure of *Don Quixote* is a parody of the
chivalric knight. When the things 'the knight of the sorrowful countenance'
sees, or thinks he ought to be seeing, do not appear that way to others, he
finds in the figure of the unseen but malevolent wizard ready-made
explanations that enable him to keep his delusions intact: if a castle looks like
an inn or a giant like a windmill, or Dulcinea like a peasant girl, it is because
his enemies have tampered with the appearance of things to deceive or
frustrate him. *Don Quixote* is an extended parody of the world which the
readers of these romance stories sought to appropriate and inhabit. Its insistent
note of irony strikes at the heart of the romantic identity to reveal the duplicity
of its seeming unity. Its aim is to destroy any foundation of trust and
conviction the readers may have had in their imaginative delusions.

Why did these romance stories have such an effect upon people? One
seemingly obvious reason would be the powerful and seductive attraction of
the identity of the chivalrous knight at that period of history. It would require
a detailed historical and cultural study to reveal the subtle complexity of this
attraction. However, the critical feature of this attraction is the way it is
mediated through the textual characteristics of the romance narratives and the
act of reading. The effect of this mediation is the power to convince the reader
of the trustworthiness of the narrative identity as the basis for affirming a
transformed self-identity; an affirmation based upon an imaginative unity
achieved at the cost of a blindness to the duplicity of rational reflection.
Although, as in the case of Don Quixote, this powerful transformation of his
self-identity initiated a process of reflection whereby every illusion is given
an explanation, there is still a suspension of reason and of continuing
interpretation. A windmill may of course be interpreted in numerous ways,
but to describe one as a giant is a clear suspension of reason. This, of course,
is Cervantes' parody upon the chivalric illusions of that period. Throughout
history to the present day there are many examples which demonstrate the
problem of the affirmation of self-identity in the act of appropriation, or the
recognition of self in a narrative. The power and attraction of the images and
configurations of such narratives influence and pervade ideals and visions in
social, political and religious contexts.

The power and attraction of the illusionary identities are revealed in the text, particularly in the relationship of prose rhythm and configuration. The power of rhythm to seduce and control consciousness and behaviour, sometimes in extreme ways is evident in the mesmerizing effect of simple, primitive rhythms. The combined effect of prose rhythm and image as the expressive mediation of the productive imagination is equally powerful in the creation of illusionary lifeworlds which foster trust and conviction. The resonance of Sonorous Being may achieve a sense of corporeal concordance at the cost of relinquishing reflection in terms of a continuing dialectical process of questioning and interpretation in relation to an open semantic horizon. This is illusionary affirmation founded upon rational duplicity; an affirmation that may lead to madness and self-destruction.

It is not that the power and attraction of such images, configurations and illusionary affirmation prevent reflection. *Don Quixote* reveals, as noted above, the way in which reflection is employed to provide explanations for the illusionary self-identities. But reflection is dominated by the imaginary identity in the sense of being separate and not dialectically related. That is, reflection is ontologically grounded in an imaginative identity, and not the otherness of narrative identity rooted in the primordial dialectic between a metaphorical second-order reference and the literal reference of discursive thought. In other words, there is a failure to allow for the mode of distanciation as defined by Ricoeur.

Consequently, reflection, which is of the order of the Same, is taken up into the imaginary world and the Self attempts to reflect upon the active state of being as though it is of the order of the Same. Because the modes of being in terms of reflection and habitation are not dialectically separated, the mode of habitation or otherness is treated as though it were of the order of the Same, since the nature of reflection is inherently of the Same. It is an attempt to reflect upon the image in terms of its objective characteristics analogous to a critique of the artistic merit of a painting in terms of the makeup of the paint. What is required of a critical appreciation of artistic merit is the imaginative appropriation of the work of art to reflect upon such aspects as light, shade, colour, etc., from the perspective of that appropriation. It is to appropriate and inhabit the perspective of the Other to reflect within that perspective, and not upon the Other. The absolute dichotomy between the Self and Other cannot be bridged by reflection, but by an imaginative appropriation of the perspective of the Other. The perspective of the Other imaginatively circumscribes the distanciation of reflection. For this reason, reflection provoked by narratives which seduce the reader to inhabit illusionary self-identities and rational duplicity is not rooted in the primordial dialectic between the Self and Other. Without the rational space, or distanciation created by this dialectic, there is a propensity to affirm unquestioned unity with a sense of absoluteness because of the dominating power of illusionary affirmation, and the suspension of a continuing rational process.

Attestation and Practical Wisdom

What is fundamental is reflection within an ontological perspective based upon the characteristics of second-order reference. It is reflection borne out of involvement and participation in particular, concrete situations. Its basis is not the universality of the word, but the semantic singularity of the sentence in its reference to particular, contextual activity. Its achievement is not the certainty of abstract analysis and deduction, but conclusions of potential availability or probability[9] grounded in an imaginative process in relating to the images and configuration of temporal activity. This view of the ontological foundation for reflection draws upon the Aristotelean notion of practical wisdom, or *phronêsis*.

In the *Nicomachean Ethics*, Aristotle is concerned with deliberation upon the practical aim of goodness, or moral excellence. In relation to this aim, how is it possible to determine the practical choice which is concerned not simply with abstract reasoning but what is right with respect to both passions and actions? According to Aristotle, deliberation is a *correctness of thinking* with regard to the particular end in view in terms of excellence. He writes,

> Excellence in deliberation in the unqualified sense, then, is that which succeeds with reference to what is the end in the unqualified sense, and excellence in deliberation in a particular sense is that which succeeds relative to a particular end. If, then, it is characteristic of men of practical wisdom to have deliberated well, excellence in deliberation will be correctness with regard to the end of which practical wisdom is the true apprehension.
> (*Nichomachean Ethics*, VI 9, 1142b, 30)

In his essay, 'Practical Reason', and the Ninth Study of *Oneself as Another*, Ricoeur develops this notion of practical reason, or practical wisdom. An important and significant characteristic of practical wisdom, analysed in the former, is the notion of reason for acting. He sets out four major features of this notion related to the category of motives which are retrospective and interpretative. That is, these are reasons which concern the retrospective intentional character of explaining, or justifying or excusing a completed action. At a more fundamental, ontological level, there is 'the intention *with which* we do something', or 'the character of desirability'. He writes,

> The idea of an order of reasons for acting is the key to practical reasoning. This reasoning has no function other than to order the 'long chain of reasons' to which the final intention has given rise. The reasoning starts from a reason for acting held to be ultimate, that is to say, one that exhausts the series of questions *why*; in other words, it starts from the character of desirability (in the broadest sense of the word, including the desire to do one's duty). It is this character of desirability that orders, regressively, the series of means envisioned to satisfy it.
> ('Practical Reason', *From Text to Action*, p. 193)

Relating this to the aim of this study, the character of desirability may be defined as an intentionality grounded in the condition of being-in-the-world. It arises from an active state of being that is driven to achieve harmony which may be considered analogous to the ethical aim of moral excellence. It is a desirability borne out of the aporias of discordant being which are explored in this study in terms of sonority. Sonority is the key expressive characteristic of active, temporal being. It is the expressive mediation of operative and particular intentionalities in the drive to achieve, in concrete, particular, active situations, the desired aim of rationally affirming a self-identity. It is the ontological grounding of reflection, or correctness of thinking, in terms of practical wisdom. It is reflection in tune with the rhythm of active being-in-the-world in a movement from discordance to concordance.

The act of conversion of self-identity in the instant of affirmation is founded upon trust in the testimony of reliable attestation. 'Reliable attestation' is the trustworthiness of testimony based upon argumentation and the witness of practical wisdom. That is, the unity of selfhood achieved with respect to argumentation of practical wisdom is not that of the unity of the Same, but the unity of being as act and power.[10] This relates to the nature of the second-order ontological reference of the imagination in terms of the textual mediation of metaphor and narrative as the power to grasp an active state of affairs.

But how is it possible to engage in argumentation to give testimony and express conviction of the achievement of the unity of being in action? 'Argumentation' is the process of reflection within the rational 'space' or distanciation created by the perspective of the Other. In the process of grasping, of imaginatively inhabiting the world of the text, the reader is provoked into continuing reflection by its configuration ontologically grounded in terms of prose rhythm. It is a questioning that is analogous to the juridical process of attempting to understand and judge the evidence in terms of the facts and stories that are related in court. It is a process of practical wisdom, of *phronêsis* which may achieve probability not certainty. This reflective process is grounded in the mediation of an active condition of being. It is the corporeal resonance of Sonorous Being dialectically related to the process of practical wisdom that brings the reader to the moment of relinquishing self-reflection in grasping the narrative identity: a moment of affirmation of the unity of identity, that in an instant is the affirmation of the unity of selfhood which immediately comes under suspicion in the detour through reflection.

In the story of 'Abraham's sacrifice' in the text of the 'Authorized Version' of the Bible, as the reader imaginatively appropriates the active world of the story which draws him towards the figurative focus of the sacrificial act, provoked into questioning by his imagination, the movement of this dialectical process is founded upon the way he is enabled imaginatively to participate in the actions of the story. It is his state of being in terms of his bodily habitation of the actions which may drive him to the moment of complete identification with the narrative's viewpoint. At that moment, the reader's self-identity is lost in the narrative. It is the moment of transcending temporality because there is a loss of consciousness of historical time. It has been relinquished on the basis of conviction and trust. The instant of this loss is the achievement of resonant concordance through the dialectical process of practical wisdom and imaginative appropriation and habitation ontologically grounded in the sonorous mediation of prose rhythm. The reader achieves the moment of understanding, of *Verstehen*,[11] which is the moment of conviction and trust. It is an hermeneutical spiral which teleologically moves towards the affirmation of a unity of active being as the foundation of *Verstehen*, and the attestation of conviction and trust. The reader grasps the meaning of the narrative from the viewpoint of Abraham's sacrificial act which affirms not a complete explanation, but an understanding based upon reasonable hope that there is a foundation for continuing reflection and enlargement of understanding.

This is not arbitrary because it is a rational process of practical wisdom based upon the achievement of conviction and trust in which, paradoxically, the reader's self-identity is at stake in the instant of relinquishing self-reflection and self-identity. It is the instant of losing and finding personal identity. Although reason is under suspicion the commitment to *reasonable hope* is the critical factor in the achievement of conviction and trust. Reasonable hope, which may be compared with Ricoeur's notion of the 'character of desirability', ensures that reflection is dialectically related to the dynamic effects of Sonorous Being in the hermeneutical spiral. In this dialectic, there cannot be a movement from discordance to concordance without the corresponding movement from suspicion to affirmation of rational understanding, and vice versa. Reasonable hope, defined as an ontological dynamic of intentionality, is the teleological characteristic of both Sonorous Being and the synthesis of the conceptual manifold. It is the dynamic of the productive imagination.

The Juridical Analogy

There are three key elements in a juridical system that are analogous to the rational interpretation of a textual narrative. These are, the commitment to the rational principle, argumentation based upon practical wisdom, and an imaginative appropriation of human actions. A commitment to the rational principle is fundamental to a juridical system which endeavours to demonstrate its rejection of arbitrary judgement. Although the system is recognized as not being free from the possibility of error, this does not detract from but strengthens the commitment. It is this commitment which informs and shapes the process and procedures of judgement by the dynamic of its motive and intention. Its aim is not conviction in terms of solution but justice which may leave the conclusion unresolved. For example, if guilt of a crime cannot be judged proven on the basis of evidence then conviction is unresolved and the accused is set free because within the process of the particular case justice prevails.

Judgement is not based upon a commitment to an abstract principle but grounded in a dialectic between argumentation of practical wisdom and the imaginative appropriation of human actions. It involves an uncompromising determination to establish empirical facts, not treated in an absolute sense, but set clearly within the context of descriptive evidence directly related to the testimony of witnesses in terms of narrative. The facts are subject to the interpretation of testimony. This is analogous to written narratives, in which the words are subject to interpretation based upon the appropriation and interpretation of the narrative. The issue is one of probability not certainty. Nevertheless the juridical process reveals that the commitment to the rational principle is rooted in the process of interpretation by argumentation in a system of advocacy. This is not limited to analysis, but is committed to rational judgement on the basis of practical wisdom. Crucially, it is founded upon concrete temporal actions, and therefore the imaginative appropriation of human action.

In the juridical system there is a rational process of understanding and explaining witnesses' narratives whereby the meaning of the crime may be grasped in terms of the 'who?' and 'why?'. It is not enough to claim understanding, there must be rational explanation in terms of argumentation and the conclusions of probability. This is analogous to reading narratives that are not imaginative flights of fantasy but imaginative habitation of lifeworlds. A reader's and a jury's appropriation and habitation are both dialectically related to the rational process of argumentation and reflection. The former is based upon a commitment to the rational principle, the latter to reasonable hope.

Sonorous Being is the ontological nature of the commitment to the rational principle, or reasonable hope expressed in the dynamic of resonance of *corporate* and *particular* intentionalities. Discordant sonority is the ontological agitation of the Self in the face of the problematic of rational unity, or the seemingly meaningless Other; it is the profound disturbance of reasonable hope as the security and teleological dynamic of the Self. Reasonable hope is the 'breath of life'. The metaphor expresses intentionality not simply as a subjective commitment but a condition of being.

Internal Dynamism of Reasonable Hope

In his study entitled, 'What Ontology in View?', Ricoeur concludes his discussion of Aristotle's *energeia* by making some brief but seemingly significant observations upon Spinoza's idea of *conatus* in the *Ethics*[12] which may shed light upon the notion of Reasonable Hope. He claims that it is in man that *conatus* is clearly readable, particularly in relation to consciousness. Acknowledging the definition of *conatus* in proposition seven of Spinoza's *Ethics*, that would seem to exclude all initiative of intention which may break with the determinism of nature,[13] *conatus*, according to Ricoeur, is the power of being of all things which in terms of man is the power to act by means of the passage from inadequate to adequate ideas. He writes,

> Thus there is a close connection between the internal dynamism worthy of the name of life and the power of intelligence, which governs the passage from inadequate to adequate ideas.
> (*Oneself as Another*, p. 316)

The idea of *conatus*, or the notion of an internal dynamism, which in one sense is pre-reflective but generated by reflection grounded in activity, relates significantly to the juridical analogy. Commitment to the rational principle which dynamically informs and shapes the system is embodied and animated by the relationship between argumentation grounded in the appropriation of activity and the imaginative grasp of the narrative. Argumentation is not reasonable because of the commitment to the rational principle, but because of the incarnation of this commitment in argumentation rooted in the appropriation of action.

This dynamism is generated by the creative relationship between two modes of being: the mode of self-reflection, and the mode of activity as the ontological engagement with the Other, a creativity that is fundamentally imaginative. It is the dynamism of reasonable hope which is the creative energy of the productive imagination enfleshed in the prereflexive relationship of the Self with its own body as its intimacy with the Other, and the consequent provocation of argumentation in terms of practical wisdom. It is the dynamism of the desire of the Self to validate its appropriation of the open horizon of the Other in a vehement affirmative act to be free of suspicion. It is, for example, to read the story of 'Abraham's sacrifice' imaginatively driven by reasonable hope that the sacrificial act is understood and, to some extent, reasonably explained. The qualifying clause, 'to some extent', implies that conviction based on the achievement of understanding does not mean complete explanation, but affirms trust in continuing interpretation and explanation; in the movement from suspicion to affirmation.

Ricoeur endeavoured to address the seemingly intractable aporias of tragic action in the quest for selfhood, particularly at the time of profound sadness in the personal tragedy of his son's death. In directing his attention to the tragedy of *Antigone*, he submits the deeply moving testimony,

> The tragedy of *Antigone* touches what, following Steiner, we can call the agonistic ground of human experience, where we witness the interminable confrontation of

man and woman, old age and youth, society and the individual, the living and the dead, humans and gods. Self-recognition is at the price of a difficult apprenticeship acquired over the course of a long voyage through the persistent conflicts, whose universality is inseparable from their particular localizations, which is, in every instance, unsurpassable.
(*Oneself as Another*, p. 243)

Through such an apprenticeship there is a tragic wisdom which is the achievement of those who refuse to contribute a 'solution' to these conflicts, and pass through, what may be a painful conversion of selfhood, a catharsis, whereby practical wisdom *responds* to tragic wisdom to reach the 'haven of conviction' beyond. Such a conversion is rooted in the discordant resonances of Sonorous Being; that the 'haven of conviction' is affirmed in a 'rhythm of hope' whereby there is a losing and finding of Self.

But there is always the suspicion that this is the haven of madness. This is a suspicion from which human beings cannot escape. Macbeth's cry of despair would seem to be an inherent, fearful disturbance of human consciousness.

> it is a tale told by an idiot, full of sound and fury,
> Signifying nothing

In his lecture, *Hamlet and Don Quixote*, Ivan Turgenev contrasts these two literary figures to reveal the nature of their madness. He describes Hamlet as the complete egocentric; the obsessively reflective person who doubts everything, including himself, and inflicts merciless suffering on himself. Turgenev finds in Don Quixote a more appealing figure of madness in his willingness to sacrifice himself. However, both suffer in a way that is destructive. Hamlet's self-reflection is not rooted in the powerful dynamic of Reasonable Hope which informs practical wisdom. Don Quixote's unconstrained hope is not subject to an apprenticeship of tragic wisdom. In both directions lie madness and self-destruction.[14] It is when reasonable hope is grounded in the rhythms of Sonorous Being that affirmation is probable.

Notes

1. See *Oneself as Another*, pp. 137–9.
2. See *Reasons and Persons*, Derek Parfit, p. 3: 'S gives to each person this aim: the outcomes that would be best for himself, and would make his life go, for him, as well as possible'.
3. See Descartes's *Discourse on Method and the Meditations*, Second Meditation.
4. The notion of 'Same' is used here in the Levinasian sense of identity (see extract from *Transcendence and Height* in *Basic Philosophical Writings*, pp. 11–20), and in particular in the way Ricoeur employs this notion in relation to *idem* – identity. (See 'The Question of Selfhood' in *Oneself as Another*, p. 18).

5.   See Richard Kearney's interview with Ricoeur, 'The Creativity of Language' in *A Ricoeur Reader: Reflection and Imagination*, pp. 468–9.

6.   Descartes's approach to certainty in terms of an epistemological foundation for knowledge was based upon his sceptical arguments in the First and Second Meditations, and his ontological argument for the existence of God in the Fifth Meditation. In the Cartesian tradition, the former have been favourably received, but the latter has been rejected. In recent debate, See Wittgenstein's *On Certainty*, in which he enunciates a number of theses about how doubt presupposes certainty.

7.   See *Oneself as Another*, p. 22.

8.   This refers to the moment of change or increase in knowledge in the process of textual interpretation. According to Ricoeur, this is closer to the logic of probability than to the logic of empirical verification (see the essay, 'The model of the text' in *Hermeneutics and the Human Sciences*, pp. 212–13). However, in his essay, 'The question of proof in Freud's writings', part III, 'Truth and Verification', he claims that the cumulative effect of validation makes proof 'probable and even convincing.' (p. 271). Verification is used in this sense with respect to the 'necessary epistemic moment' that ensures the hermeneutical circle is not vicious.

9.   The notion of probability is a key feature which has been implicit and at times explicit in the development of the analysis in this study. In this final chapter, there is an attempt to complete the analysis with respect to the critical importance of attestation in relation to probability. The analysis draws closely upon Ricoeur's work in which there is also a development of this notion which has its roots in Aristotle's *Rhetoric*. At the beginning of *The Rule of Metaphor*, he writes: '*Rhetoric* is the treatise containing the equilibrium between two opposed movements, one that inclines rhetoric to break away from philosophy, if not to replace it, and one that disposes philosophy to reinvent rhetoric as a system of second-order proofs. It is at this point, where the dangerous power of eloquence and the logic of probability meet, that we find rhetoric stands under the watchful eye of philosophy. It is this deep-seated conflict between reason and violence that has plunged the history of rhetoric into oblivion ...' (p. 12). Plato played a powerfully influential role in this separation and decline of the importance of the art of persuasion in claiming, incorrectly according to Ricoeur (see also Michael Gagarin's essay, 'Probability and Persuasion' in *Persuasion: Greek Rhetoric in Action*, ed. Ian Worthington), that the early Rhetoricians placed probability above truth. Ricoeur also attempts to show that metaphor was reduced to a single figure of speech, and in consequence the dynamic of metaphoric displacement involving the sentence and whole discourse was lost in the traditional western substitutional theory of metaphor. The effect of the neglect or loss of the integral relationship of the logic of probability and metaphor in the separation of the poetic and rational modes of discourse was the consequent loss of the crucial importance of second-order proofs in philosophy. Ricoeur's concern to reunite the poetic and rational modes of discourse in a dialectical relationship is pursued in development of his hermeneutical philosophy. In his essay, 'The model of the text', in *Hermeneutics and the Human Sciences*, the nature of second-order proofs is taken up in the contrast of validation to verification. He writes, 'As concerns the procedures of validation by which we test our guesses, I agree with Hirsch that they are closer to a logic of probability than to a logic of verification ... Validation is an argumentative discipline comparable to the juridical procedures of legal

interpretation. It is a logic of uncertainty and of qualitative probability' (p. 212). He is, however, aware of the danger of the hermeneutical circle being a vicious circularity, and the need to show that an interpretation must be more probable than another. He states, 'There are criteria of relative superiority which may easily be derived from the logic of subjectivity' (p. 231). It is apparent in relation to the latter that this leads to his work on the notion of attestation, particularly in *Oneself as Another.* (For a helpful study on this notion, see Jean Greisch's essay, 'Testimony and Attestation' in *Paul Ricoeur: The Hermeneutics of Action*, ed. Richard Kearney.) Attestation is a central theme of this final chapter which attempts to demonstrate that it is not based upon the logic of subjectivity, but the logic of *Sonorous Being.*

10. See Ricoeur's interpretation of Aristotle's concepts of *dunamis* and *energeia* in section 2 of the tenth study of *Oneself as Another*, pp. 303–17.

11. *Verstehen* was first developed as a method of understanding in hermeneutical philosophy by Dilthey and has since become a key concept in the developments of this branch of philosophy. See Ricoeur's essay, 'The task of Hermeneutics' in *Hermeneutics & the Human Sciences.*

12. See *Oneself as Another*, pp. 315–17.

13. *Oneself as Another*, p. 316.

14. In *Points ... Interviews, 1974–1994*, Derrida is recorded as saying, '... a certain 'madness' *must* keep a lookout over every step, and finally watch over thinking, as reason does also?' (p. 363). Is this kind of madness the madness of the self keeping a lookout over the self keeping a lookout over the self keeping a lookout over the self ... as the self is deconstructed and disseminated? In contrast, in the continuing hermeneutic founded upon the primordial dialectic between 'suspicion' and 'affirmation' the latter may be the moments of the dying and resurrection of self in the manner of George Herbert's poem *Mortification*, 'That all my dyings may be life in death'.

Chapter 9

A New Metaphysics

A New Metaphysics – Sonorous Being

Throughout this study, one of my main concerns has been to address the metaphysical assumptions which I referred to in the early part of Chapter 1; that is, the seemingly unquestioned assumptions in Kantian and Cartesian rationalism, in Husserlian phenomenology, and even in Heideggerian ontology revealed in the 'we' of the text. It is these assumptions which imply a metaphysical closure upon the problem of presence. A foundation is postulated transcending temporality, and, consequently, there is an explicit or implied assumption that presence is affirmed in an actual or potential grasp of the absolute unity of the appearance of the thing-itself. In contrast, my attempt has been to take the 'given', in terms of a phenomenological, linguistic perspective, by showing that the metaphysical grounding of the affirmation of presence is mediated in and through the imaginative grasp of the narrative mode of language. It is a grounding that gives rise to reasonable hope that the affirmation of presence is achieved in terms of the probability of rational meaning of the narrative.

I concluded Chapter 8 with the statement that reasonable hope is grounded in the rhythms of Sonorous Being. It is in the ontological rhythmic resonance of the Self's appropriation of the Other's perspective upon the *lebenswelt* of a narrative that reasonable hope of the affirmation of presence, with respect to the Self's identity, is grounded. The act of the imaginative appropriation is a dynamic movement, mediated by the prose rhythm of the text, whereby the text is transcended. The Self is grounded not in transcendental subjectivism founded upon *a priori* metaphysical Kantian categories, or the Cartesian rational subject, or Husserlian intentionality, but in the ontological patterned resonance set up by the dialectical relationship between the Self and Other in relation to the text mediated by the givenness of the textual rhythmic structure. There is a rhythmic resonance, a trembling, in the reader's condition of being with the probability of losing and finding, relinquishing and affirming self-identity in the Other's viewpoint. In the instant of the loss of self, affirmation is teleologically sustained by an ontological rhythmic dynamism, and the dialectic between suspicion and affirmation of self-identity is transcended. Sonorous Being may therefore be understood in a metaphysical sense. It is a metaphor[1] of the transcendental grounding that is imaginatively appropriated by means of the givenness of textual narratives.

A Radical Change in Metaphysical Perspective

The radical difference between this metaphysical grounding of human reason and the traditional Western approach to metaphysics is the perspective that is taken with respect to the Other. The epistemological desire to understand has been directed towards the acquisition of knowledge of the Other. It has been an attempt to know the unknowable. In terms of the notion of truth in Western philosophy, Levinas writes,

> The theory of knowledge is a theory of truth. Like Parmenides of Plato it poses the question: how can the absolute being manifest itself in truth? For to be known, it must manifest itself in the world where error is possible. How can a being, subject to error, touch the absolute being without impairing its absolute character?
> ('Martin Buber and the theory of knowledge', *The Levinas Reader*, p. 60)

It is my concern to show that it is not a question of an epistemological grasp of the Other, but an appropriation of the Other's viewpoint; to stand, as it were, in the place of the Other and view the world from that perspective. It is in the appropriation of that viewpoint that there is a metaphysical grounding of human reason in an hermeneutical process open to the horizon of reasonable hope. In the instant of appropriation, when there is a losing and finding of self, the transcendental grounding is the resonance of Sonorous Being corporeally mediated by the rhythmic structure of the text.

The Power of Appearance: Care and Deinon

In Chapter 3, I made reference to Ricoeur's interpretation of Aristotle's treatment of the concepts of *dunamis* and *energeia* in the *Metaphysics* with respect to action and the notion of being, to show that this notion may include the rhythmic resonance of Sonorous Being. In other words, the imaginative appropriation and habitation of a lifeworld is a dynamic, active movement of the Self grounded in a rhythmic condition of being. In *Oneself as Another*, Ricoeur develops his ontology of selfhood in terms of the central characteristic of action by relating his interpretation of Aristotle's *energeia–dunamis* to Heidegger's notion of Care (*Sorge*). He writes,

> One could, it is true, confine oneself to comparing a limited group of Aristotelian concepts to their Heideggerian counterparts and interpret the former in relation to the latter. In this way, the comparison between *Sorge* in Heidegger and *praxis* in Aristotle could occasion a deeper understanding of both concepts. For my part, I am all the more attentive, as it has been the Aristotelian concept of *praxis* that helped me to widen the practical field beyond the narrow notion of action in terms of analytic philosophy; in turn, Heideggerian *Sorge* gives to Aristotelian *praxis* an ontological weight that does not seem to have been the major intention of Aristotle in his *Ethics*. (*Oneself as Another*, p. 311)

Since *Care* is Heidegger's basic notion of the structure of *Dasein* with respect to its being made visible, its appearance, its presence in the world, following Ricoeur, it is the ontological characteristic of action which is the dynamic intentionality of *Sorge* and the presence of selfhood. Presence is grounded in the potentiality of being in terms of an ontological understanding of *praxis*, or the Heidegerrian notion of Care.

In Heidegger's analysis of being in *An Introduction to Metaphysics*, a clearer ontological understanding of Care may be gained, particularly with regard to the dynamic resonance of the fundamental existential question of being, which I have already touched upon in Chapter 4.[2] In his commentary on the first chorus from Antigone of Sophocles, which forms part of chapter four, 'The Limitation of Being', he meditates upon the Greek poetic grasp of being-human. At the beginning of the poem, man is encompassed by one word, *deinotation*, the strangest. Heidegger translates this word to mean, terrible. He writes,

> The *deinon* is the terrible in the sense of the overpowering power which compels panic fear, true fear; and in equal measure it is the collected, silent awe that vibrates with its own rhythm.
> (*An Introduction to Metaphysics*, p. 149)

The fundamental question of being, which is to be understood ontologically and not epistemologically, looms in moments of existential anxiety or fear rooted in the hidden power of Sonorous Being. It is essentially a condition of being-in-the-world which ontologically reverberates with the fundamental question and its relationship of Care with the world. In the thrownness of *Dasein*, the terrible sense of the overpowering power, the *deinon*, gives rise to an ontological, dynamic impulse of Care directed towards the world in a rhythmic resonance of appearance, of presence.

This *deinon* is the power which drives the movement of affirmation in the appropriation of a narrative identity in the instant of losing and finding self-identity. It is manifested in the existential, corporeal trembling of this instant when the dialectic of affirmation and suspicion is transcended. *Deinon* is released by the dialectical relationship between Self and Other as the reader, in the instant, is driven to inhabit the viewpoint of the Other, the implied author, of the narrative. By means of this power, the reader's imaginative grasp of the narrative, and consequently the 'space' for rational understanding and explanation, is rooted in the transcendental ground of Sonorous Being. It is the rhythmic structure, the prose rhythm, of the narrative which initiates the process of release transcending the givenness of the text. The rhythmic, corporeal trembling in the instant of affirmation is the manifestation of the metaphysical grounding of Sonorous Being. It is a grounding which resonates with the power of affirmation, but which does not close the hermeneutical process. The instant of affirmation of self-identity, in the losing and finding of self, transcends the hermeneutical cycle and the dialectic between Self and

Other, between suspicion and affirmation. But the instant of affirmation, sustained by the *deinon* of Sonorous Being, although transcending the hermeneutical cycle, is released within the cycle which is immediately and insistently reinstated by this ontological power which drives it.[3] The metaphysical grounding of Sonorous Being does not therefore affirm an absolute unity of rational meaning, but a teleological impulse of affirmation which maintains the dialectic of affirmation and suspicion.

Beyond the Familiar

The transcendental instant of affirmation may be understood in Heideggerian terms as the surpassing of the limit of the familiar. As he meditates upon the poet's grasp of being-human, of man, as *deinon*, and the overpowering power translated as strange, he is concerned to make clear that this is not strangeness as an impression that the powerful makes upon us. He writes,

> But man is strangest of all, not only because he passes his life amid the strange understood in this sense (that is, to be cast out of the 'homely') but because he departs from his customary, familiar limits, because he is the violent one, who tending toward the strange in the sense of the overpowering, surpasses the limit of the familiar.
> (*Ibid.*, p. 151)

This is a striving beyond the familiar driven by the ontological overpowering power, *deinon*. The Other's perspective upon the lifeworld of the narrative is beyond the familiar of the reader in his or her striving to inhabit that perspective.

It is a striving for appearance, for the affirmation of the presence of self-identity. Heidegger writes,

> We shall fully appreciate this phenomenon of strangeness only if we experience the power of appearance and the struggle with it as an essential part of being-there.
> (*Ibid.*, p. 151)

The constant struggle of being-human is *Dasein* as appearance. It is to appropriate the instant of self-affirmation, the unity of self-identity, the presence of self. Above all else, it is in the reading of narratives that this is given the probability of reasonable hope, because the imaginative habitation of the narrative is a dialectical process between Self and Other whereby the power to go beyond the familiar in the losing and finding of self is released by the rhythmic structure of the text. It is this structure which mediates the resonance of Sonorous Being, the source of this transcendental power. The dialectical movement of the Self towards being lost in the Other trembles as the struggle to take the hermeneutical leap of affirmation is driven by the growing intensity of the transcendental power of Sonorous Being.

Deinon and Configuration

Heidegger's meditation upon *deinon* provides further clarity to this hermeneutical movement with respect to its configuration by the Self's imaginative grasp of the Other's viewpoint. *Deinon* is the unitary relationship between two things: *technē*, which he interprets as knowledge in the sense of the passion, the power to bring a work of art into being, and not as the result of observation of previously unknown data; and *dikē*, which is the power that imposes the governing structure upon the stability of the familiar.[4] *Deinon* is the interrelationship between *technē* and *dikē*, and the struggle between them, that being-human is driven to appear, to be present in the world. According to Heidegger, *technē* can never master *dikē*, and so man is tossed back and forth between structure and the structureless, between the affirmation and suspicion of rational meaning.[5] In terms of the hermeneutical cycle, *deinon*, being-human, is the dialectic between Self and Other, and it has been my aim in this study to show that it is only when the dialectic of *deinon* is transcended that the unitary interrelationship between its two traits of *technē* and *dikē* is overcome in the instant of affirmation of the presence of the Self in the world.

Apprehension, Ingathering and Prose Rhythm

The means of this overcoming, according to Heidegger, is apprehension (*Vernehmung*) which he defines as three things: a decision, and not a mere process; as having an essential relationship with the logos; and logos as the essential foundation of language, and as such it is a struggle and the ground on which man's historical being-there is built.[6] It is, therefore the struggle for appearance. In terms of man's relationship with textual narratives, apprehension may be understood as the Self's decision to appropriate, to inhabit the narrative identity, and overcome the familiar in an instant of affirmation of self-presence.

It is the relationship of apprehension and logos that is of particular significance with respect to the act of configuration and its rhythmic dynamic released by Sonorous Being mediated by the prose rhythm of the text. Heidegger is concerned to make clear that the key characteristic of logos is ingathering. He writes,

> Ingathering means here: to collect oneself amid dispersion into the impermanent, to recapture oneself out of confusion in appearance. But this gathering that is still a turning-away can be accomplished only through the gathering which is a turning-to, which draws the essent into togetherness of being. Thus logos as ingathering becomes a need <Not> and parts from logos in the sense of togetherness of being (*physis*). It is *logos* as ingathering, as man's collecting-himself toward fitness <Fug>, into homelessness, insofar as the home is dominated by the appearance of the ordinary, customary, and commonplace.
> (*Ibid.*, p. 169)

I have attempted to show that it is the rhythm of textual narratives which is the fundamental characteristic of the linguistic mode. Rhythm therefore is the dynamic of this ingathering, understood as the act of configuration, driven by the ontological vehemence of corporeal intentionality grounded in Sonorous Being. As the reader struggles to inhabit the lifeworld of the narrative, her familiar world, to which her self-identity clings, is wrested from its security by the increased rhythmic trembling in the instant of letting go in the habitation of the unfamiliar. It is in this instant that the presence of Self is affirmed by the rhythmic ingathering of Sonorous Being.

The Postmodern World and a New Metaphysics

The problem in Western philosophy, which, for the most part, has been the assumed metaphysical grounding of rational meaning, is the way in which this grounding has inhibited, or enslaved the existential freedom of being-human. There has been an implicit propensity to collude with the Self's attempt to hold fast to the familiar.[7] In contrast, the concern of contemporary philosophers to lay bare the illusion of linguistic affirmation of presence, and abandon any metaphysical grounding, often fails to fully address the power of the terrible as the Self is driven to be human beyond the familiar. For example, conventional meaning, as a basis for pragmatism, is torn asunder by this power, and the Self may be driven to madness. Even with Derrida, the disturbing question is, what happens when deconstruction has dislodged all metaphysical securities?

Historically, it is a time for a new metaphysics. The old securities are being fragmented, and the temptation to reaffirm them leads not only to illusions of freedom in the desire to be human, but dangerous dogmatisms which cause suffering and destruction. The euphoria of philosophers like Jean-François Lyotard, who concludes *The Postmodern Condition* with the appeal,

> Let us wage war on totality; let us be witnesses to the unpresentable; let us activate the differences and save the honour of the name.
> (*The Postmodern Condition*, p. 82)

is fundamentally an appeal for protest rather than a concern for the challenge of a new metaphysics; a concern for a grounding of being-human in reasonable hope as the power of the terrible drives the Self beyond the familiar.

My aim in this study has been to show that it is in the human imaginative capacity to tell stories, and particular in the way these stories have been given a textual mode, that a metaphysical grounding is mediated. All textual narratives present the opportunity whereby the Self may be driven beyond the familiar, especially those narratives such as the biblical story of Abraham's sacrifice of Isaac, in which the power of the terrible threatens an ontological disturbance expressed in discordant, corporeal trembling, but is sustained into a rhythmic resonance of concordance and reasonable hope. The metaphysical grounding is Sonorous Being as the Self is driven by the power of the terrible to a losing and finding beyond the familiar in the presence of the Other.

In this age of fragmentation, the role of textual narratives is fundamental in historical interpretation and redescription in relation to the losing and finding of renewed identities; that is, identities that may be secure in the relationship with the Other, and open to the semantic horizon beyond the familiar, able to relate to the insecurity posed by the threat of suspicion as an inherent characteristic of the dialectic between Self and Other. The quality of textual narratives does of course vary, particularly with respect to the story and the textual mediatory rhythmic structure. In simple terms, many narratives do not drive the reader beyond the familiar but often collude with illusion or fantasy in the manner of the chivalric stories of the time when Cervantes wrote *Don Quixote*. My analysis of the Abrahamic narrative in the 'Authorized Version' of the Bible is an attempt to show that the rhythmic structure of such texts have the mediatory capacity to activate the reader's imagination to sustain a losing and finding of self-identity in relation to the Other. It is an attempt to show that textual narratives can and do have refined rhythmic structures that mediate a metaphysical grounding in Sonorous Being.

Judaic-Christian Narrative Tradition

The Abrahamic story of the sacrifice of Isaac is a principal narrative in the Judaic-Christian tradition which is essentially a narrative tradition.[8] Although my aim in this study is not to consider the part that this tradition may play in this postmodern world, I would nevertheless propose that there is a need to examine this tradition in the light of a new metaphysical perspective based upon the notion of Sonorous Being. It is significant that the theological implications may be discerned in this narrative tradition in the story of Moses and the Burning Bush. The disturbance of Moses' self-identity has already taken place in the clash between his Egyptian and Hebraic roots. But in his encounter with the divine presence at Mount Horeb, he is driven, in fear and trembling, beyond the familiar; driven beyond the securities of those cultures, even in a condition of conflict, which have given a level of ontological stability to his self-identity; driven by a power of terrible strangeness to encounter the Other. In that encounter his cry for security in terms of knowledge of the Other is denied. He cannot know the unknowable, the I AM THAT I AM. He is called to inhabit the perspective of the Other and take up the role of bringing that perspective to bear upon the historical experience of bondage.[9] His resistance to go beyond the familiar in clinging to the security of his self-identity, in terms of his inability to take on the mantle of leadership, is overcome as his being trembles and is sustained by a power that resonates with the harmony of a renewed identity.

The narrative reveals the ontological rhythmic resonance that lies at the heart of the Judaic- Christian tradition; a tradition which is essentially narrative in textual mode. The Hebraic linguistic rhythms of this tradition manifest the presence of this ontological resonance. In the consequent historical developments of this tradition, these have reverberated in other languages through the translations made by those who have entered deeply into its ontological resonance. The 'Authorized Version' in the English language is a supreme example. The problem with many modern translations is the dominance of a concern for explanation over understanding grounded in the rhythms of Sonorous Being.[10] There is a failure imaginatively to inhabit, to enter deeply, the rhythmic structures of the original language in appropriating the perspective of the Other in terms of narrative identity.

This is the cultural malaise of the postmodern world. The discarding of the grand narratives which grounded reflection and rational explanation in corporate rhythms of the cultural milieu has deprived language of its ontological roots. The epistemological aspiration in the Western world to know the unknowable has finally succumbed to the illusion of the sovereignty of objectivity.[11] In the struggle for emancipation from the restrictions of these grand narratives, and the consequent social corruptions and injustices, the aspiration to know the unknowable and control human destiny has dulled and deprived people of linguistic rhythmic sensitivities leading to a failure to search for the ground of a new metaphysics.

For this to be so, there must be an awakening to the experience of the poetic, to the music of language; a stirring of those ontological predispositions towards the rhythms of the soul. This calls for a prolonged process of the refining of aesthetic sensibilities in the endeavour to encounter the presences in literature, music and art. In his book, *Real Presences*, George Steiner makes a moving and powerful appeal for a renewed receptivity of the poetic. In doing so, he expresses his concern for the risk of muddle and embarrassment when attempting to tell of what happens inside oneself in the experience of art, music and literature. He writes,

> The psychological and social fact that ours is an age in which embarrassment terrorizes even the confident and the lonely has sharpened the inhibitions. Structuralist semiotics and deconstruction are expressions of a culture and a society which 'play it cool'. These are potent rationalizations. At the close of this argument I want to suggest that they mask a more radical flinching; that the embarrassment we feel in bearing witness to the poetic, to the entrance into our lives of the mystery of otherness in art and in music, is of a metaphysical-religious kind.
> (*Real Presences*, p. 178)

To overcome these inhibitions and embarrassment there must be a freeing of the imagination through the stimulus of fear and wonder in the decision and willingness to go beyond the familiar to encounter the awesome strangeness of the Other. It is an awakening of human freedom through the pulse of narrative experienced as an ontological trembling at the edge of the unknown. But, in religious terms, this trembling is the disturbance of an encounter with what Steiner calls 'the strangeness of evil or the deeper strangeness of grace'. The ontological reverberation of discordance threatens disintegration of the human psyche, but the power of *deinon* released by the dialectic between Self and Other through the mediation of the rhythmic structure of the narrative can transform discordance into concordance and the harmony of the human soul in its encounter with the Other.

When John Keats called this life 'a vale of soul-making',[12] he was of course referring to the total experience of life, and especially the suffering that is endured. And yet, that image was an expression of his poetic sensibilities and powerful imagination which had been nurtured over many years. Although we cannot aspire to his poetic genius, it is the rhythms of the soul that are refined in this vale. The Judaic-Christian narrative tradition possesses the mediatory linguistic givenness of a cultural setting for this vale in the richness of its textual narratives included in the corpus of its literature. The challenge is to enter more deeply into this heritage free, to whatever extent is possible, from any predisposition to traditional metaphysical securities; to inhabit and appropriate its corporate ontological rhythms. Through the process of such habitation there may be the refinement of the imagination and aesthetic sensibilities releasing the power of Sonorous Being in an encounter with 'the strangeness of evil and the deeper strangeness of grace' beyond the limit of the familiar.

Notes

1. This is a metaphor of the condition of the Other in terms of transcendental grounding, in contrast to the traditional metaphors of Western metaphysics which are metaphors of the Other. With the illusion of gaining knowledge of the Other they are treated as concepts.
2. See Chapter 4, pp. 00–00.
3. That is, released by the power of *deinon* working through the productive imagination in relation to the givenness of linguistically structured consciousness, mediated by rhythmic phonicity and objective, corporeal, rhythmic resonance, whereby the mediation of the transcendental grounding of Sonorous Being is achieved in the *instant* of affirmation.
4. See *An Introduction to Metaphysics*, pp. 165–7.
5. Unless this relationship is determined by the primordial dialectic, as defined in this study, within an hermeneutical cycle open to an horizon of reasonable hope, affirmation is grounded in illusions, and the structureless is predisposed to anarchy and chaos.
6. *Ibid.*, pp. 167–9.
7. Heidegger identifies this propensity with the change in the original meaning of the Greek word for essent, *physic*, in the translation to the Latin, *natura*. In consequence, the original meaning, which embraced the fundamental question of

being, 'is thrust aside, and the actual philosophical force of the Greek word is destroyed' (*An Introduction to Metaphysics*, p. 13). The 'familiar' became the powerful lifeworlds of the Roman Empire, Christendom and medieval society.

8.   See *The Poetics of Biblical Narrative*, Meir Sternberg.

9.   The perspective of divine revelation in the biblical narrative is always contextual and historical. See *Theology of the Old Testament*, Walther Eichrodt Volume 1, Chapters 6 and 7.

10.   See 'the concept of Enlightenment' in *Dialectic of Enlightenment*, Theodor Adorno and Max Horkheimer.

11.   For example, see Introduction to the New English Bible, p. xvi, 'The translator must often go behind the traditional text to discover the writer's meaning'.

12.   See extract from letter quoted in *John Keats*, Robert Gittings, p. 261.

Bibliography

Abrahams, Nicholas. *Rhythms.* Collected and presented by Nicholas T. Rand and Maria Torok. Trans., Benjamin Thigpen and Nicholas Rand. Stanford: Stanford University Press, 1995.

Ackerill, J.L., ed. and trans. *A New Aristotle Reader.* Oxford: Clarendon Press, 1987.

Adorno, Theodor and Horkheimer, Max. *Dialectic of the Enlightment.* London & New York: Verso, 1979.

Allison, Henry. E. *Kant's Transcendental Idealism.* New Haven and London: Yale University Press, 1983.

Aristotle. *Poetics,* translation (with Greek text) and critical notes by S.H. Butcher included in *Aristotle's Theory of Poetry and Fine Art.* Also a prefatory essay, 'Aristotelian Literary Criticism' by John Gassner. New York: Dover Publications, Inc., 4th edn, 1951.

————. *The Art of Rhetoric.* Trans., intro. and notes by H.C. Lawson-Tancred. Penguin Books, 1991.

Baum, P.F. *The Principles of English Versification.* Cambridge, Mass.: Harvard University Press, 1922.

Baugh, Albert C. and Cable, Thomas. *A History of the English Language.* London: Routledge, 1993.

Beardsley, Monroe C. *Aesthetics: Problems in the Philosophy of Criticism.* New York: Harcourt, Brace & Co., 1958.

Beistegui, Miguel de. *Heidegger and the Political.* London and New York: Routledge, 1998.

Benjamin, Walter. *Illuminations.* Ed. and intro. Hannah Arendt. Trans. Harry Zohn. Fontana, 1973 (translated from original 1955).

Bergson, Henri. *Creative Evolution.* Trans. A. Mitchell. London: Macmillan, 1928.

Black, Matthew and Rowley, H.H., eds. *Peake's Commentary on the Bible.* London: Nelson, 1962.

Black, Max. *Models and Metaphors: Studies in Language and Philosophy.* Ithaca: Cornell University, 1962.

Bleicher, Josef. *Contemporary Hermeneutics.* London and New York: Routledge, 1980.

Bloom, Harold, *et al. Deconstruction and Criticism.* New York: Continuum, 1979.

Bradbury, Malcolm. *The Modern British Novel.* Penguin Books, 1993.

Bradley, A.C. *Oxford Lectures on Poetry.* New York: Macmillan St Martin's Press, 1965.

Byron, William. *Cervantes.* London: Cassell, 1978.

Caputo, John D. *The Prayers and Tears of Jacques Derrida.* Bloomington & Indianapolis: Indiana University Press, 1997.

Cassirer, Ernst. *The Philosophy of Symbolic Forms.* 3 vols. Trans. R. Manheim. New Haven: Yale University Press, 1957.

——. *Language and Myth.* Trans. Suzanne K. Langer. New York: Dover Publications Inc., 1953.

Caygill, Howard. *A Kant Dictionary.* Oxford: Blackwell, 1995.

Cervantes, Miguel de. *Don Quixote.* Trans. J.M. Cohen. The Penguin Classics, 1950.

Clark, Kenneth. *Looking at Pictures.* London: John Murray, 1972.

Clark, S.H. *Paul Ricoeur.* London and New York: Routledge, 1990.

Coleridge, Samuel Taylor. 'Biographia Literaria' in *Selected Poems and Prose.* Ed. Stephen Potter. London: The Nonesuch Press, 1962.

Conrad, Joseph. *Heart of Darkness.* Penguin Modern Classics, 1973.

Critchley, Simon. *The Ethics of Deconstruction.* Oxford: Blackwell, 1992.

Croxall, T.H. *Kierkegaard Commentary.* London: James Nisbet & Co. Ltd, 1956.

Curley, Edwin, ed. and trans. *A Spinoza Reader: The Ethics and Other Works.* Princeton: Princeton University Press, 1994.

De Man, Paul. *The Resistance to Theory.* Minneapolis: University of Minnesota Press, 1986.

——. *Blindness and Insight.* 2nd edn. London: Routledge, 1983

Derrida, Jacques. *Speech and Phenomena.* Trans. and intro., David B. Allison. Evanston: Northwestern University Press, 1973.

——. *Of Grammatology.* Trans. Gayatri Chakravorty Spivak. Baltimore and London: The John Hopkins University Press, 1976.

——. *Writing and Difference.* Trans. and intro. and additional notes, Alan Bass. London: Routledge, 1978.

——. *Margins of Philosophy.* Trans. with additional notes, Alan Bass. London: Harvester Wheatsheaf Press, 1982.

——. *Of Spirit.* Trans. Geoffrey Bennington and Rachel Bowlby. Chicago and London: The University of Chicago Press, 1989.

——. *Points...* Ed. Elisabeth Weber. Trans. Peggy Kamuf and Others. Stanford: Stanford University Press, 1995.

——. *The Gift of Death.* Trans. David Willis. Chicago and London: The Chicago University Press, 1995.

——. 'The Retrait of metaphor', *Enclitic*, 2.2, 1978.

——. Derrida Interview: 'Deconstruction of Actuality'. *Radical Philosophy 68*, Autumn 1994.

Descartes, René. *Discourse on Method and the Meditations.* Trans. and intro. F.E. Sutcliffe. Penguin Classics, 1968.

Dillistone, F.W., ed. *Myth and Symbol.* Essay: 'The Religious Symbol', Paul Tillich. London: SPCK, 1966.

Dillon, M.C. *Merleau-Ponty's Ontology.* 2nd edn. Evanston: Northwestern University Press, 1977.

Dilthey, Wilhelm. *Selected Writings.* Ed. H.P. Rickman. Cambridge: Cambridge University Press, 1976.

Douglas, J.D. *et al.*, eds. *The New Bible Dictionary.* London: The Inter-Varsity Fellowship, 1962.

Dyson, A.E. and Lovelock, Julian. *Masterful Images.* London and Basingstoke: The Macmillan Press, 1976.

Ebor, Donald. Chairman of the Joint Editorial Committee. *New English Bible.* Oxford University Press and Cambridge University Press, 1970.

Eichrodt, Walter. *The Theology of the Old Testament*, Vol. 1, trans. J.A. Baker. Bloomsbury Street London: SCM Press Ltd, 1961.

Eliot, T.S. *The Complete Poems and Plays.* London: Guild Publishing, 1969.

————. *On Poetry and Poets.* London: Faber and Faber Ltd, 1957.

————. *The Use of Poetry and Criticism.* London: Faber and Faber Ltd, 1964.

Erikson, E. 'Identity and the Life Cycle'. *Psychological Issues, Monograph 1, 1959.*

Fitzgerald, F. Scott. *The Great Gatsby.* Penguin Books, 1975.

Fóti, Véronique M. *Heidegger and the Poets.* New Jersey: Humanities Press, 1992.

Freire, Paulo. *The Pedagogy of the Oppressed.* Trans. Myra Bergman Ramos. Penguin Books, 1972.

Frye, Northrop. *The Great Code.* London, Melbourne & Henley: Routledge & Kegan Paul, 1982. *Anatomy of Criticism.* Penguin Books, 1957.

Gadamer, Hans-Georg. *Truth and Method.* Trans. and revised Joel Weinsheimer and Donald G. Marshall. 2nd revised edn. London: Sheed and Ward, 1993.

Gebauer, Gunter and Wulf, Christopher. *Mimesis.* Trans. Don Reneau. Berkeley and Los Angeles: University of California Press. 1995.

Gittings, Robert. *John Keats.* Penguin Books, 1979.

Goodman, Nelson. *Languages of Art: An Approach to the Theory of Symbols.* Indianapolis: Hackett Publishing Co., 1976.

————. *Ways of Worldmaking.* Indianapolis: Hackett Publishing Co., 1978.

Hamilton, Paul. *Coleridge's Poetics.* Oxford: Blackwell, 1983.

Hand, Séan, ed. *The Levinas Reader.* Oxford UK & Cambridge USA: Blackwell, 1989.

Hardy, Thomas. *Poems of Thomas Hardy.* Selection and intro. T.R.M. Creighton. London: Macmillan, 1974.

————. *The Return of the Native.* London: Macmillan, 1974.

Harvey, David. *The Condition of Postmodernity.* Oxford: Blackwell, 1989.

Hahn, Lewis Edwin, ed. *The Philosophy of Paul Ricoeur.* Chicago and La Salle, Illinois: Open Court, 1995.

Hawkes, Terence, *Metaphor.* London & New York: Routledge, 1972.

Hawthorn, Jeremy. *A Concise Glossary of Contemporary Literary Theory.* 2nd edn. London: Edward Arnold, 1994.

Hayman, Ronald. *Leavis.* London: Heinemann, 1976.

Heaney, Seamus. *Preoccupations.* London: Faber & Faber, 1980.

Hegel, G.W.F. *Science of Logic.* Trans. A.V. Miller. Atlantic Highlands: Humanities Press International, Inc., 1989.

————. *The Encyclopaedia Logic.* Trans. T.F. Geraets, W.A. Suchting and H.S. Harris. Indianapolis Cambridge: Hackett Publishing Co. Inc., 1991.

Heidegger, Martin. *Being and Time.* Trans. John Macquarrie and Edward Robinson. Oxford: Blackwell, 1962.

————. *An Introduction to Metaphysics.* Trans. Ralph Manheim. Hew Haven & London: Yale University Press, 1987.

————. *The Basic Problems of Phenomenology.* trans. and intro. Albert Hofstadter. Bloomington & Indianapolis: Indiana University Press. 1988.

————. *The Concept of Time.* Trans. William Neil. Oxford: Blackwell, 1992.

————. *Basic Writings.* Ed. and intro. David Farrell Krell. London: Routledge, 1993.

————. *The Principle of Reason.* Trans. Reginald Lilly. Bloomington & Indianapolis: Indiana University Press, 1996.

Henn, T.R. *The Bible as Literature.* London: Lutterworth Press, 1970.

Herbert, George. 'Mortification' included in *Complete Works of George Herbert*, London: Nelson and Sons, 1860. Also included in *The Metaphysical Poets.* Penguin Books, revised edn, 1966.

Hobsbaum, Philip. *Metre, Rhythm and Verse Form.* London & New York: Routledge, 1996.

Hopkins, Gerard Manley. *Poems and Prose.* Selected and ed. W.H.Gardner. Penguin Books, 1963.

Husserl, Edmund. *Logical Investigations.* Vol. 1. Trans. J. Findlay. London & Henley: Routledge & Kegan Paul, 1977

————. *Origin of Geometry.* An Introduction by Jacques Derrida. Trans. with preface and afterword by John P. Leavey, Jr. Lincoln and London: University of Nebraska Press, 1989.

————. *On the Phenomenology of the Consciousness of Internal Time (1893–1917).* Trans. John Barnett Brough. Dordrecht, Boston & London: Kluwer Academic Publishers, 1991.

————. *Cartesian Meditations.* Intro.and trans. Dorion Cairns. Dordrecht, Boston & London: Kluwer Academic Publishers, 1995.

Jameson, Fredric. *The Prison-House of Language.* Princeton: Princeton University Press, 1972.

Kamuf, Peggy, ed. *A Derrida Reader: Between the Blinds.* London: Harvester Wheatsheaf, 1991.

Kant, Immanuel. *Critique of Pure Reason.* Trans. Norman Kemp Smith. London: Macmillan, 1929, second impression, 1933.

————. *Critique of Judgment.* Trans. Werner S.P luhar. Indianapolis/Cambridge: Hackett Publishing Co., 1987.

————. *Critique of Practical Reason.* Trans. Lewis White Beck. 3rd edn. New York: Macmillan, 1993

————. *Prolegomena to Any Future Metaphysics.* Ed. Beryl Logan. London & New York: Routledge, 1966. 'The Only Possible Argument in Support of a Demonstration of the Existence of God.' in Cambridge Ed.I, *Theoretical Philosophy 1755–1770.* Trans. David Walford in collaboration with Ralf Meerbote.

Kearney, Richard. *Poetics of Imagining.* London: Harper Collins *Academic,* 1991.

————. ed, . *Paul Ricoeur: The Hermeneutics of Action.* SAGE Publications, 1996.

———— and Rainwater, Mara. *The Continental Philosophy Reader.* London & New York: Routledge, 1996.

Kierkegaard, Søren. *Journals 1834–1854.* Trans. Alexander Dru. Fontana Books, 1958.

————. *The Concept of Dread.* Trans. Walter Lowrie. Princeton: Princeton University Press, 1957.

————. *Philosophical Fragments.* Original trans. David Swenson, revised Howard V. Kong. Princeton: Princeton University Press, 1967.

————. *Fear and Trembling.* Trans. Alistair Hannay. Penguin Books, 1985.

Kim, Jaegwon and Sosa, Ernest. *A Companion to Metaphysics.* Oxford: Blackwell, 1995.

Kisiel, Theodore. *The Genesis of Heidegger's Being and Time.* Berkeley and Los Angeles: University of California Press, 1995.

Kittay, Eva Feder. *Metaphor.* Oxford: Clarendon Press, 1987.

Kofman, Sarah. *Nietzsche and Metaphor.* Trans. Duncan Large. London: The Athlone Press, 1993.

Kraut, Richard, ed ed. *The Cambridge Companion to Plato.* Cambridge: Cambridge University Press, 1992.

Langan, Thomas. *Merleau-Ponty's Critique of Reason.* New Haven: Yale University Press, 1966.

Laplanche, Jean. 'Psychoanalysis as anti-hermeneutics'. *Radical Philosophy 79.* Sept/Oct 1996.

Lawler, Leonard. *Imagination and Chance.* State University of New York Press, 1992.

Lear, Jonathan. *Aristotle: The Desire to Understand.* Cambridge: Cambridge University Press, 1988.

Leavis, F.R. *The Great Tradition.* Penguin Books, 1972.

————. *D.H. Lawrence: Novelist.* Penguin Books, 1973.

Levinas, Emmanuel. *Totality and Infinity.* Trans. Alphonso Lingis. Pittsburgh: Duquesne University Press, 1961.

————. *The Theory of Intuition in Husserl's Phenomenology.* 2nd edn. Evanston: Northwestern University, 1995.

————. *Basic Philosophical Writings.* Ed. Adriaan T. Peperzak, Simon Critchley and Robert Bernasconi. Bloomington & Indianapolis: Indiana

University, 1996.

Lyotard, Jean-François. *The Postmodern Condition.* Trans. Geoff Bennington and Brian Massumi. Manchester: Manchester University Press, 1984.

MacCormac, Earl R. *A Cognitive Theory of Metaphor.* Cambridge, Mass.: The MIT Press, 1990.

MacIntyre, Alisdair. *After Virtue.* 2nd edn. London: Duckworth, 1985.

Manguel, Alberto. *A History of Reading.* London: Flamingo, Harper Collins Publishers, 1997.

Martinich, A.P., ed. *The Philosophy of Language.* 3rd edn. New York and Oxford: Oxford University Press, 1996.

Matustík, Martin J. and Westphal, Merold, eds. *Kierkegaard in Post/Modernity.* Bloomington and Indianapolis: Indiana University Press, 1995.

Merleau-Ponty, Maurice. *Phenomenology of Perception.* Trans. Colin Smith. London and Henley: Routledge & Kegan Paul, 1962. (Translation of *Phénoménologie de la perception*, original 1945.)

———. *Signs.* Trans. and intro. Richard C. McCleary. Evanston: Northwestern University Press, 1964. (Translation of *Signes*, original 1960.)

———. *The Visible and the Invisible.* Ed. Claude Lefort. Trans. Alphonso Lingis. Evanston: Northwestern University Press, 1968. (Translation of *Le Visible et l'invisible*, original 1964.)

———. *The Prose of the World.* Trans. John O'Neill. Evanston: Northwestern University Press, 1973. (Translation of *La Prose du monde*, original 1969.)

Nash, Cristopher, ed. *Narrative in Culture.* London & New York: Routledge, 1994.

Newman, J.H. *Newman's University Sermons.* London: SPCK., 1970.

Nietzsche, F. 'On Truth and Lies in a Nonmoral Sense' in *Philosophy and Truth.* Trans. and ed. Daniel Breazeale. Atlantic Highlands, New Jersey: Humanities Press, 1979.

Norris, Christopher. *What's Wrong with Postmodernism.* London: Harvester Wheatsheaf, 1990.

Nussbaum, Martha C. *Love's Knowledge.* New York and Oxford: Oxford University Press, 1990.

Painter, George D. *Marcel Proust*, Penguin Books, 1990.

Parfit, Derek. *Reasons and Persons.* Oxford: Oxford University Press, 1986.

Pavel, Thomas. *The Feud of Language.* Cambridge: Blackwell, 1989.

Pearce, T.S. *Literature in Perspective: T.S. Eliot.* London: Evans Brothers Ltd, 1967.

Peperzak, Adriaan. *To the Other.* West Lafayette: Purdue University Press, 1993.

———, ed. *Ethics as the First Philosophy.* New York and London: Routledge, 1995.

Polkinghorne, John. *Reason and Reality.* London: SPCK, 1991.

Proust, Marcel. *Remembrance of Things Past.* 3 vols. Trans. C.K. Scott Moncrieff and Terence Kilmartin. Penguin Books, 1983.

Quennell, Peter. *A History of English Literature*, London: Ferndale Editions, 1979.

Rad, Gerhard von. *Genesis: A Commentary.* London: SCM Press Ltd, 1961.

Reagan, Charles E., *Paul Ricoeur: His Life and His Work.* Chicago and London: The University of Chicago Press, 1996.

Reeves, James. *Understanding Poetry.* London: Pan Books Ltd, 1965.

Richards, I.A. *The Philosophy of Rhetoric.* Oxford: Oxford University Press, 1936.

―――. *Principles of Literary Criticism*, London: Routledge, 1967.

Paul Ricoeur's works (English translations):

Ricoeur, Paul. *Freedom and Nature: The Voluntary and Involuntary.* Trans. and intro. E.V. Kohak. Evanston: Northwestern University Press, 1966. (Translation of *Le volontaire et l'involontaire*, original 1950.)

―――. *Husserl: An Analysis of His Phenomenology.* Translation of several articles, intro. E.G. Ballard and L.E. Embree. Evanston: Northwestern University Press, 1967.

―――. *History and Truth.* Trans. and intro. Charles A. Kelby. Evanston: Northwestern University Press, 1965. (Translation of several articles included in *Histoire et vérité*, original 1955.)

―――. *Fallible Man.* Trans. Charles A. Kelby. Intro. Walter A. Lowe. New York: Fordham University Press, 1986. (Translation of *L'homme faillible*, original 1960.)

―――. *The Symbolism of Evil.* Trans. E. Buchanan. New York: Harper and Row, 1967. (Translation of *La symbolique du mal*, original 1960.)

―――. *Freud and Philosophy.* Trans. Denis Savage. Newhaven and London: Yale University Press, 1970. (Translation of *De l'interprétation. Essai sur Freud*, original 1965.)

―――. *The Conflict of Interpretations.* Trans. by D. Hyde *et al.* Evanston: Northwestern University Press, 1974. (Translation of *Le conflit des interprétations. Essai d'hermeneutique*, original 1969.)

―――. *The Rule of Metaphor.* Trans. R. Czerny, K. McLaughlin and J. Costello. London: Routledge & Kegan Paul, 1978. (Translation of *La métaphore vive*, original 1975.)

―――. *Hermeneutics and the Human Sciences.* Ed. and trans. J.B. Thompson. Cambridge: Cambridge University Press, 1981. (Translation of various essays originally published between 1973 to 1979.)

―――. *Time and Narrative.* 3 vols. Trans. K. McLaughlin and D. Pellauer. Chicago and London: The University of Chicago Press, 1984. (Translation of *Temps et récit*, original Vol. I, 1983, Vol. II, 1984, Vol. III, 1985.)

―――. *From Text to Action.* Trans. K. Blamey and J.B. Thompson. London: Athlone Press, 1991. (Translation of *Du texte à l'action. Essai d'hérméneutique, II*, original 1986.)

————. *Oneself as Another.* Trans. Kathleen Blamey. Chicago and London: The University of Chicago Press, 1992. (Translation of *Soi-meme comme un autre*, original 1990.)

————. *A Ricoeur Reader: Reflection and Imagination,.* Ed. Mario J. Valdés. London: Harvester Wheatsheaf, 1991. (Including translations of various essays, and interviews in English.)

————. *Critique and Conviction. Conversations with Francois Azouvi and Marc de Launay.* Trans. Kathleen Blamey. Polity Press, 1998.

Rorty, Richard. Contingency, Irony and Solidarity. Cambridge University Press, 1989.

Sacks, Sheldon, ed. *On Metaphor.* Chicago: The University of Chicago Press, 1979.

Sallis, John. *Delimitations.* Bloomington and Indianapolis: Indiana University Press, 1995.

Saussure, Ferdinand de. *Course in General Linguistics.* Trans. and annotated by Roy Harris. Ed. Charles Bally and Albert Sechehaye with the collaboration of Albert Reidlinger. London: Duckworth, 1983.

Schapiro, Leonard. *Turgenev.* Oxford: Oxford University Press, 1978.

Scully, James, ed. *Modern Poets on Modern Poetry.* Fontana Collins, 1966.

Slade, Tony. *Literature in Perspective: D.H. Lawrence*, London: Evans Brothers Ltd, 1969.

Smith, Barry and Woodruff Smith, David, eds. *The Cambridge Companion to Husserl.* Cambridge University Press, 1995.

Silverman, Hugh J, ed. *Postmodernism – Philosophy and the Arts.* New York and London: Routledge, 1990.

Soskice, Janet Martin. *Metaphor and Religious Language.* Oxford: Clarendon Press, 1985.

Steiner, George. *The Death of Tragedy.* London: Faber and Faber, 1963.

————. *No Passion Spent.* London: Faber and Faber, 1996.

————. *Real Presences.* London: Faber and Faber, 1991.

Steiner, Peter. *Russian Formalism.* Ithaca: Cornell University Press, 1984.

Sternberg, Meir. *The Poetics of Biblical Narrative.* Bloomington: Indiana University Press, 1987.

Stevenson, Randall. *Modernist Fiction.* London: Harvester Wheatsheaf Press, 1992.

Studdert-Kennedy, G.A. 'The Suffering God' in *The Unutterable Beauty.* Hodder and Stoughton, 1947.

Svenbro, Jesper. *Phrasikleia: An Anthropology of Reading in Ancient Greece.* Trans. Janet Lloyd. Ithaca: Cornell University Press, 1993.

Tillich, Paul. *Theology and Culture.* New York: Oxford University Press, 1964.

Trask, R.L. *A Dictionary of Phonetics and Phonology.* London and New York: Routledge, 1996.

Traversi, Derek. *T.S. Eliot: The Longer Poems.* London: The Bodley Head, 1976.

Trigg, Roger. *Reality and Risk*. 2nd edn. London: Harvester Wheatsheaf, 1989.

Walker, Ralph C.S. 'Verificationism, Anti-realism and Idealism'. *European Journal of Philosophy*. Vol. 3, No. 3, December 1995.

Warner, Martin, ed. *The Bible as Rhetoric*. London and New York: Routledge, 1990.

Wittgenstein, Ludwig. *Philosophical Investigations*. Trans. G.E.M. Anscombe, Blackwell, 1968.

Wood, David, ed. *Derrida: A Critical Reader*. Oxford: Blackwell, 1992.

———. *On Paul Ricoeur: Narrative and Interpretation*. Ed. David Wood. London and New York: Routledge, 1991.

Wordsworth, William. Preface to the 'Lyrical Ballads', *Poetical Works*. Ed. Thomas Hutchinson and revised Ernest de Selincourt. London: Oxford University Press, 1936.

Worthington, Ian, ed. *Persuasion: Greek Rhetoric in Action*. London and New York: Routledge, 1994.

Yeats, W.B. 'Among School Children' in *Poems of W.B. Yeats*. Selected, with an introduction by A. Norman Jeffares, Macmillan, 1984.

Appendix

Prose Rhythm of Abraham's Sacrifice of Isaac in the 'Authorized Version' of the Bible

/   – dominant stress
~   – light stress
---   – cadence

```
                        //              ~              //      ~
Genesis|22:1  And it came to pass after these things, that God did tempt Abraham,
        ~               //        ~           //        ---
              and said unto him, Abraham: and he said, Behold, here I am.

              ~         //      ~        ~           //
Genesis|22:2  And he said, Take now thy son, thine only son Isaac, whom thou
        //          //          --------------------
              lovest, and get thee into the land of Moriah;

              //      ~        ~             //              ~
              and offer him there for a burnt offering upon one of the mountains
              -------------
              which I will tell thee of.

                        //                   ~              //
Genesis|22:3  And Abraham rose up early in the morning, and saddled his ass,
              //              ~              ~
              and took two of his young men with him, and Isaac his son,
              //            ------------------------
              and clave the wood for the burnt offering,
              //                   ~              ------------------
              and rose up, and went unto the place of which God had told him.
                        ~                   /      ~        /          -----
Genesis|22:4  Then on the third day Abraham lifted up his eyes, and saw the place
              --------
              afar off.

                 ~              ~           /              ~
Genesis|22:5  And Abraham said unto his young men, Abide ye here with the ass;
                           ~              /          -------------------------
              and I and the lad will go yonder and worship, and come again to you.
```

153

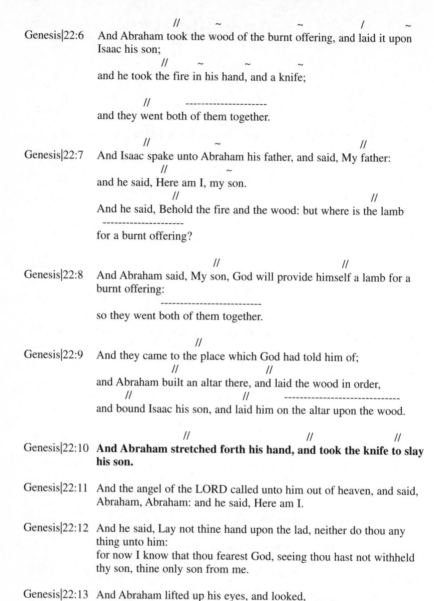

Genesis|22:6   And Abraham took the wood of the burnt offering, and laid it upon Isaac his son;

and he took the fire in his hand, and a knife;

and they went both of them together.

Genesis|22:7   And Isaac spake unto Abraham his father, and said, My father:

and he said, Here am I, my son.

And he said, Behold the fire and the wood: but where is the lamb

for a burnt offering?

Genesis|22:8   And Abraham said, My son, God will provide himself a lamb for a burnt offering:

so they went both of them together.

Genesis|22:9   And they came to the place which God had told him of;

and Abraham built an altar there, and laid the wood in order,

and bound Isaac his son, and laid him on the altar upon the wood.

Genesis|22:10   **And Abraham stretched forth his hand, and took the knife to slay his son.**

Genesis|22:11   And the angel of the LORD called unto him out of heaven, and said, Abraham, Abraham: and he said, Here am I.

Genesis|22:12   And he said, Lay not thine hand upon the lad, neither do thou any thing unto him:
for now I know that thou fearest God, seeing thou hast not withheld thy son, thine only son from me.

Genesis|22:13   And Abraham lifted up his eyes, and looked,
and behold behind him a ram caught in a thicket by his horns:
and Abraham went and took the ram, and offered him up for a burnt offering in the stead of his son.

Genesis|22:14   And Abraham called the name of that place Jehovahjireh:
as it is said to this day, In the mount of the LORD it shall be seen.

Genesis|22:15 And the angel of the LORD called unto Abraham out of heaven the
second time,

Genesis|22:16 And said, By myself have I sworn, saith the LORD,
for because thou hast done this thing,
and hast not withheld thy son, thine only son:

Genesis|22:17 That in blessing I will bless thee,
and in multiplying I will multiply thy seed as the stars of the heaven,
and as the sand which is upon the sea shore;
and thy seed shall possess the gate of his enemies;

Genesis|22:18 And in thy seed shall all the nations of the earth be blessed;
because thou hast obeyed my voice.

Genesis|22:19 So Abraham returned unto his young men,
and they rose up and went together to Beersheba;

Index